# Programming and Problem-Solving

## *Key Concepts and Program Structures*

First Edition

## David A. Freitag

First Edition 2019

10 9 8 7 6 5 4 3 2 1

Printed in the United States of America

ISBN: 9781709458118

Imprint: Independently published

*Dedicated to students who have an enthusiasm and passion for learning.*

# Contents

Preface ........................................................................................................... 13

Introduction .................................................................................................... 15


Chapter 1  Software Development ................................................................... 17

Chapter 2  Learning Computer Science .......................................................... 21

Chapter 3  Solving Problems .......................................................................... 25

Chapter 4  Variables and Constants ............................................................... 39

Chapter 5  Modules and Functions ................................................................. 53

Chapter 6  Decision Structures and Boolean Logic ....................................... 77

Chapter 7  Loops ............................................................................................. 99

Chapter 8  Input Validation ........................................................................... 123

Chapter 9  Arrays .......................................................................................... 133

Chapter 10   Object-Oriented Programming .................................................. 145

Chapter 11   Solving a Problem Step-by-Step .............................................. 163


Appendix A:  Index and Glossary .................................................................. 185

Appendix B:  Problem-Solving Roadmap ...................................................... 193

Appendix C:  Test Plan Checklist .................................................................. 195

Appendix D:  Program Checklist .................................................................... 197

Appendix E:  Checklist of Coding Concepts .................................................. 199

Appendix F:  Using Computer Science Tutors ............................................... 201

Appendix G:  Tutoring Computer Science Students ...................................... 203

Appendix H:  Pseudocode to Java Examples ................................................ 205

Appendix I:  Pseudocode to Python Examples .............................................. 207

# Detailed Contents

Preface ....................................................................................................................13

Introduction ..........................................................................................................15

Chapter 1  Software Development ........................................................................17
    Software Development Job Titles ...................................................................18
    Is Software Development for you? ..................................................................19
    Are you going to be a successful student? .....................................................20

Chapter 2  Learning Computer Science ................................................................21
    Computational Thinking .................................................................................22
    Detail Orientation ..........................................................................................24
    Some Ideas to Remember ..............................................................................24
    Review Questions ...........................................................................................24

Chapter 3  Solving Problems ................................................................................25
    Have a Plan to Solve the Problem..................................................................25
    Expectations ...................................................................................................26
    Your Intent......................................................................................................27
    What before How ...........................................................................................28
    Talk Out Loud.................................................................................................28
    Problem-Solving Techniques .........................................................................29
    Syntax and Logic Errors.................................................................................30
    Testing ............................................................................................................31
    Debugging.......................................................................................................33
    Test Plans.......................................................................................................34
    Boundary Conditions .....................................................................................36
    Are You Stuck? ...............................................................................................36
    Review Questions ...........................................................................................37

**Chapter 4  Variables and Constants**..................................................................**39**

Terminology You must Know..................................................................39

Sample Pseudocode..................................................................39

Variables and Constants ..................................................................40

Naming Standards ..................................................................40

Declaring Variables and Constants ..................................................................42

Displaying Output ..................................................................42

Getting Input ..................................................................43

Formulas ..................................................................44

Input, Processing, and Output ..................................................................45

How to Write a Program..................................................................46

Programming and Problem Solving ..................................................................49

Design and then Code..................................................................50

Review Questions ..................................................................51

Can You Do This? ..................................................................52

**Chapter 5  Modules and Functions** ..................................................................**53**

Terminology You must Know..................................................................53

Sample Pseudocode..................................................................54

Modules..................................................................54

Arguments and Parameters..................................................................55

Functions ..................................................................56

Naming Standards ..................................................................57

Contents of a Module or Function..................................................................58

Scope ..................................................................59

Common Mistakes..................................................................60

Passing Data to a Module or Function..................................................................64

Hierarchy Charts ..................................................................65

IPO Charts ..................................................................66

Analysis and Programming ..................................................................67

Library Functions ..................................................................67

Developing a getRandomNumber Function ..................................................................68

Generalized Modules and Functions ..................................................................70

Evolution of Generalized Input Functions: Part 1 ..................................................................73

Program Structures: IPO with Modules and Functions ..................................................................74

Review Questions ..................................................................................................... 75

Can You Do This? .................................................................................................... 76

**Chapter 6 Decision Structures and Boolean Logic** ...................................................... **77**

Terminology You must Know ....................................................................................... 77

Sample Pseudocode .................................................................................................. 77

Relational Operators ................................................................................................. 78

Logical Operators ..................................................................................................... 80

Common Boolean Errors ............................................................................................ 81

Common Errors ........................................................................................................ 82

Comparing Strings .................................................................................................... 84

The If-Else-If statement ............................................................................................. 85

The Select-Case Structure: Creating a Menu ............................................................... 87

Modulus ................................................................................................................. 89

Evolution of Generalized Input Functions: Part 2 – Checking for Invalid Data ................ 90

Removing Code from Main .......................................................................................... 92

Answers to Exercises in this Chapter .......................................................................... 94

Review Questions ..................................................................................................... 96

Can You Do This? .................................................................................................... 97

**Chapter 7 Loops** .......................................................................................................... **99**

Terminology You must Know ...................................................................................... 100

Sample Pseudocode ................................................................................................. 100

A Counting Loop ..................................................................................................... 100

A Loop with a Sentinel Value .................................................................................... 101

An Input While-Loop with a Sentinel Value ................................................................. 102

A wantsToContinue Loop .......................................................................................... 103

For-Loops .............................................................................................................. 104

Nested Loops ......................................................................................................... 105

A Game Loop ......................................................................................................... 106

Removing Code from Main or a Module ...................................................................... 108

Evolution of Generalized Input Functions: Part 3 – Looping when Invalid Data is Entered....110

Displaying a Shape .................................................................................................. 112

Building a Multiplication Table ................................................................................... 113

Problem Solving ..................................................................................................... 116

Review Questions ..................................................................................................117

Can You Do This? ................................................................................................118

**Chapter 8  Input Validation** ...........................................................................**123**

Terminology You must Know..............................................................................123

The Standard Input Validation Models ...........................................................123

One-function Input Validation Model ..............................................................124

Two-function Input Validation Model ..............................................................125

Validating String Data ......................................................................................127

Common Input Values .......................................................................................128

Review Questions ..............................................................................................129

Can You Do This? ..............................................................................................130

**Chapter 9  Arrays** .............................................................................................**133**

Terminology You must Know..............................................................................134

One-Dimensional Arrays ..................................................................................135

Two-Dimensional Arrays ..................................................................................137

Initializing an Array with Random Unique Values ........................................139

Key Array Skills .................................................................................................141

Review Questions ..............................................................................................142

Can You Do This? ..............................................................................................143

**Chapter 10  Object-Oriented Programming** ...................................................**145**

OOP Terminology ..............................................................................................145

Classes and Objects .........................................................................................146

Constructors ......................................................................................................147

Getters and Setters...........................................................................................148

Inheritance ........................................................................................................149

Overriding a Method ........................................................................................151

Overloading a Method......................................................................................152

Unified Modeling Language (UML) .................................................................153

Accessing an Object .........................................................................................154

A Full OOP Example .........................................................................................154

Review Questions ..............................................................................................160

Can You Do This? ..............................................................................................161

**Chapter 11  Solving a Problem Step-by-Step**............................................................**163**

    Can You Do This? .....................................................................................182


**Appendix A:  Index and Glossary**.......................................................................**185**

**Appendix B:  Problem-Solving Roadmap** ..........................................................**193**

**Appendix C:  Test Plan Checklist**.......................................................................**195**

**Appendix D:  Program Checklist** ........................................................................**197**

**Appendix E:  Checklist of Coding Concepts** ......................................................**199**

**Appendix F:  Using Computer Science Tutors** ...................................................**201**

**Appendix G:  Tutoring Computer Science Students** ..........................................**203**

**Appendix H:  Pseudocode to Java Examples** .....................................................**205**

**Appendix I:  Pseudocode to Python Examples** ..................................................**207**

# Preface

Why do so many students fail their first and only computer science class? There is no doubt some students do not spend the time required to understand the subject. Some students don't do the reading at all, hoping they can sneak through the class unnoticed and, unsurprisingly, fail the class. But many students do the reading, spend the time, and still fail the class. Why *is* that?

One reason computer science students fail is that their textbook tries to be exhaustive and includes too much material for beginning students to absorb. The instructor compensates by only using half of the textbook, and only covering half of the information in the chapters that are used. It may not be clear to the student what, out of all the information in the textbook, needs to be learned to pass the course. Students can become confused and frustrated with the class and their instructor when their textbook contains too much information for a beginning student.

Another reason for student failure is that most textbooks ignore the thought processes used by programmers in solving problems. Those textbooks introduce a new concept, present a problem, and then expect the student to connect different concepts together in solving the problem.

This textbook starts at the beginning and shows the thought processes used to solve problems. The goal for this textbook is to remove the mystery by covering only what a student needs to know to pass a first-semester course such as *Computer Science 101*, or *Introduction to Programming and Problem Solving*. If the student can answer the review quesitons and complete all the "Can You Do This?" exercises at the end of each chapter, then the student is ready to move onto the next chapter. There are not 20 exercises after each chapter, there are only a few critical exercises the student must be able to complete. The student does not have to guess what they need to know—this textbook tells them exactly what they need to know and no more.

------------

It is unfortunate for students, and for society in general, that there is a shortage of qualified computer science instructors. Because of that, many schools try to force most of their students out of the Computer Science department after the first class.

The first programming course in many universities contains hundreds of students—which only shows the desirability of entering the job market with a Computer Science degree. What students don't know is that the first computer science course in college is designed to fail or force out most of them. Many colleges cannot allow a class of 400 students to pass their first course in computer science and move on to the next course. The university doesn't have the capacity or the teachers for 400 eager students in the second, third and later semesters.

Designing the first class to weed out anyone without any background in logical thinking has the unintended consequence of weeding out educationally disadvantaged students who could have learned logical thinking if they were only given a chance. The stereotypical male programmer continues to dominate the Computer Science industry due to the lack of teaching capacity of schools, colleges, and universities and most corporations' lack of interest in changing the situation.

This textbook tries to make first-semester concepts easy to learn and available to all. Everyone should have the opportunity to learn computational thinking and how to solve computational problems by focusing on organizing their thoughts, performing structured thinking, following known problem-solving techniques, and paying attention to the details. All students should have the opportunity to learn to generalize patterns and algorithms to solve a variety of problems using computational thinking techniques. To help as many students as possible, this textbook demonstrates how to *think* about a problem before writing one line of code. By following the patterns and examples, students will be able to write decent code after finishing this book.

------------

This book uses pseudocode that should be understandable to anyone learning C, C++, Java, Python, JavaScript, C#, or any language in the C-family of software languages. Why use pseudocode? Because it is language-independent. Because requiring pseudocode exposes those areas the student does not know. Many students hate pseudocode because of this—it exposes them as posers when they don't know the material. Good programmers who know their stuff can talk about code using pseudocode. If you can't say *what* you are trying to code in pseudocode, you can't code it in Java, Python, C, C++, C# or any other software language.

All that said, Computer Science is not an easy subject to master without effort. If a student has breezed through school up to now and expects to breeze through their first computer science course, they may be in for a rude shock. If a student believes smart students don't have to study, then that student is setting themselves up to fail. Learning to program and solve problems takes sustained and consistent effort. Fortunately, it is an effort that can be fun and enjoyable.

There is no doubt most students *can* succeed in this field if they stay with it, work hard, and endeavor to think clearly. After all, this isn't rocket science.

*"It goes against the grain of modern education to teach children to program. What fun is there in making plans, acquiring discipline in organizing thoughts, devoting attention to detail and learning to be self-critical?"* *

*—Alan Perlis*

* It's actually lot's of fun! (and profitable)

# Introduction

Computer Science is an exciting field that is still growing. There are many opportunities for people with skills in programming and problem-solving. Good high-paying jobs will be available for skilled software developers and analysts for the foreseeable future.

You may not know this, but your first programming class is be an introduction to computational thinking and problem solving, not in writing code. Not everyone will be a professional programmer in the future, but almost everyone will need to solve problems using computational thinking. Beginning software developers don't realize it's very difficult to write code when you don't know how to think about the problem properly.

Many students want to learn to program. The good news is that most programming concepts are not all that hard to learn. The bad news is that there are a lot of them. And you can't forget any of them—you will never know when a concept or technique is just the solution to the problem you are working on.

To be a programmer you have to pay attention to what you are learning and what you are doing. You have to watch your mind as you solve problems. What? Yes, self-awareness of your thoughts is a key to getting better at solving problems in computer science, biology, architecture, ROTC, and in every other field of study.

> Don't be fooled by the myth of the genius who says, "Eureka!" and solves the problem. Real genius lies in the work a person is willing to do before the "Eureka!" moment.

Perhaps you think programmers are arrogant loners who write code all day. Not so. Programmers must meet and communicate with peers, supervisors, managers, clients, and users. Great communication skills will take you farther in your career than superb coding skills. If you are taking a class in-person, use this time to improve your communication and speaking skills. Volunteer for EVERYTHING. Raise your hand.

Who do you think earns letters of recommendation from their instructors? Who do you think gets hired? Who do you think earns the promotion? Who do you think is assigned the most interesting work?

This is who: the person who puts themselves out there trying to help their teacher, their manager, their peers, their customers, their clients, and their company. The person who raises their hand—that's who. And that person can be you!

> This book is all about learning to think, solve problems and write software to solve problems. To be successful you have to read, study, memorize concepts when necessary, and write lots of code. There is no way around that. You have to practice.

Do basketball or football players practice between games? Of course they do. And yet many (failing) computer science students try to pass their courses by only writing code for required assignments and during an exam. To succeed you have to practice just as an athlete does between games. You have to practice thinking and coding so you can show what you can do at crunch time on exam day.

## IF YOU ARE A STUDENT AT A UNIVERSITY...

Basic rule-of-thumb: For every credit hour of a difficult class, spend 3 times the number of credit hours per week on that class.

So, if you are using this book in a **4 credit hour** class, that means you should spend an active and focused 12 hours per week outside of class on reading, studying, and completing assignments. Let's look at the math:

3 times 4 credit hours = **12 hours per week**
(and more than 12 hours if you struggle with the material)

At 7 days per week: 12 hours per week = 1:40 every day

At 5 days per week: 12 hours per week = 2:25 every day

If you miss only ONE day,

At 7 days per week: spend 3:20 the next day to catch up

At 5 days per week: spend 4:50 the next day to catch up

Are you willing to do that? Not many students are.
As you can see, you have to keep up—you can't miss one day!

Some students think only incompetent people must study or practice, but they are wrong. Every professional athlete and software developer has spent thousands of hours learning, practicing, and perfecting their craft. Their secret is they enjoy the process so it doesn't seem like work to them. Don't fall for the myth of the lazy genius. Work hard and people will start to think you're a genius. I hope this textbook will help you to learn to work hard in solving problems and have fun doing so!

# Chapter 1
# Software Development

Software developers can work almost anywhere. Can you think of a job that doesn't use a computer or a phone app in some way? Well, someone had to write code to make that computer do something.

Where programmers work includes:

- Universities, community colleges, high schools, and all other types of schools
- Corporate Information Technology departments (IT)
- Large software companies like Microsoft, Google, Oracle, Apple, and Amazon
- Small service firms that focus on web design, games, or business applications
- Consulting companies who work with all kinds of businesses
- Organizations like hospitals, insurance companies, airports, and retailers
- Local, state, and federal government
- Any company that produces a product containing a microprocessor

Many students are interested in game development and there are many, many software developer positions in companies that produce games. Here are a few types:

- Game Engine Programmers
- Artificial Intelligence Programmers
- Graphics Programmers
- Network Programmers
- Physics Programmers
- Tools Programmers
- User Interface Programmers
- Animation Programmers
- And more!

If you work for yourself, or for a smaller company, you will be responsible for many roles. Sometimes you will be an analyst, sometimes a physics programmer, a researcher, a graphic designer, or a sound engineer. If you work for a large company you may be able to specialize and focus on one of those areas.

## Software Development Job Titles

Here are some job titles related to programming and software development:

| | |
|---|---|
| Developer | Programmer |
| Software Engineer | Web Developer |
| Mobile Application Developer | AI Software Engineer |
| Network Engineer | Database Administrator |
| UNIX Network Administrator | Systems Analysts |
| Data Warehouse Analyst | Business Intelligence Analyst |
| Data Security Analyst | Business Analyst |
| Quality Assurance Analyst | Release Delivery Analyst |
| Social Media Analyst | Web Designer |
| Systems Architect | Data Modeler |
| Network Architect | Network Security Analyst |
| Quality Assurance Tester | Technical Writer |
| Trainers | IT Auditor |
| Technical Sales Support | Technical Support |
| Graphic Artist | Implementation Analysts / Consultants |
| System Integration Analyst / Consultants | Account Managers |
| Project Managers | Application Development Manager |
| Chief Security Officer | Chief Technology Officer |
| Data Warehouse Manager | Business Intelligence Manager |
| Quality Assurance Manager | Release Manager |

You may not know what many of those jobs are but, as you take classes and read about the field, you may find an area that interests you enough to make a career of it.

Consider meeting with a career counselor or a computer science academic advisor to explore your options. You can also look at job postings on-line for companies you might dream of working for someday and see what skills and degrees they are expecting their applicants to have.

*"Any fool can write code that a computer can understand. Good programmers write code that humans can understand."*

—*Martin Fowler*

## Is Software Development for you?

Everyone is different, but most people who succeed in a field of study have certain common traits. Either they are born with them (lucky them!), or they have to learn them. If software development is for you, you will recognize yourself in the below descriptions, or you will want to develop these traits.

- You enjoy solving puzzles.
- You pay attention to the details.
- You don't give up when the solution is not obvious.
- You feel challenged to work harder when you cannot solve the problem quickly.
- You are an active learner who takes responsibility for your education.
- You realize that learning takes effort. You know you can't skate by this subject with little effort.
- You know you have to work hard at computer science to learn it.
- You are able to recognize and follow already established patterns. You don't try to reinvent concepts that have already been invented long, long ago.
- You enjoy learning and using best-practices.
- You enjoy learning by reading about the subject.
- You enjoy learning something new every day of your career.
- Between semesters or on weekends you write code, or design programs, or read about computer science—because you enjoy it!

If the above qualities don't describe you, and you have no intention of developing those qualities, then you should put this book down and find a field of study that excites you and makes you want to work weekends on it. Life is too short and college is too expensive to get an education in a subject you don't enjoy.

If you don't have the above qualities now, but you think you might be able to develop them, then continue with your studies in computer science. You may discover you love it. Or you may decide it is not for you. Either way, you have learned something valuable about your interests.

*"When I am working on a problem, I never think about beauty but,*
*when I have finished, if the solution is not beautiful, I know it is wrong."*
*—R. Buckminster Fuller*

## Are you going to be a successful student?

Successful students in Computer Science commit to doing these activities:

- Keep up with the reading.
- Work hard to understand the concepts covered in each chapter.
- Ask for help when they are stuck or confused by a concept.
- <u>Never</u> pretend to know something they don't know.
- Be engaged and focused in class at ALL times.
- Participate and ask questions in class.
- Start their assignments well before the due dates.
- <u>Never</u> start an assignment the day it is due.
- Never ask or expect a tutor to write code for them.
- Never waste time Googling a concept since the answer is already in the textbook.
- Solve the problem away from the computer before trying to write code.
- Turn in code that works and follows established best-practices in program design.
- Understand that code that runs and works, could still receive a zero on the assignment if it does not follow the required structure and restrictions.
- Know that **you can do this** when you give yourself enough time and apply what you know.

Too many students self-sabotage themselves by starting too late or giving up too soon. If you cannot commit to doing the above, then you will struggle in this and in any field. Find a field of study in which you are excited and thrilled. Don't waste your time, your fellow students' time, and your teacher's time if you don't want to be here.

Are you still here? Good! Keep reading!

> *"Our greatest weakness lies in giving up. The most certain way to succeed is always to try just one more time."*
> —*Thomas Edison*

> *"Five percent of the people think;*
> *ten percent of the people think they think;*
> *and the other eighty-five percent would rather die than think."*
> —*Thomas Edison*

*Computer scientists are in the 5% group!*

# Chapter 2
# Learning Computer Science

Computer science is not programming. But programming is part of computer science—as is problem-solving. In an introductory textbook like this you will get a smattering of ideas about Computer Science, but by no means is it complete. As you continue your education you will learn more about the subject. This book is only a place to begin.

Learning anything new can be tough. Learning to write code is learning a new language: you have to learn syntax, grammar, and ways to do things that are specific to the language. You have to be able to translate English to Pseudocode, Java, Python, C, C++, C#, or some other programming language.

And I have what might be bad news for you: working as a programmer means solving word problems that use math. There may or may not be a correct answer. Nobody can do your work for you. After you graduate from school, every program you write will be new and will never have been done before. You can't Google the answer. That's why programmers are paid the big bucks—they have learned to think in ways most people don't. Your job as a student of computer science is to change the way you think to be more efficient and effective in solving problems related to computer science.

> *"It should be mandatory that you understand computer science."*
> *—will.i.am*

If you are a good problem solver, and you know a programming language, you have the opportunity to write good code. Good code has several qualities:

- It runs correctly and has NO bugs.
- It is readable and understandable, even by inexperienced programmers.
- It is short, but not so short as to be confusing.
- It is well-written, even in areas nobody will ever see.
- It uses established programming patterns.
- It is indented properly and uses blank lines appropriately.
- It is organized into modules and functions.
- It is well documented.
- It is reusable.

This is your goal. Now let's start learning how to get there.

## Computational Thinking

Any programming class is an education in computational thinking. Here is one way to organize the concept of computational thinking:

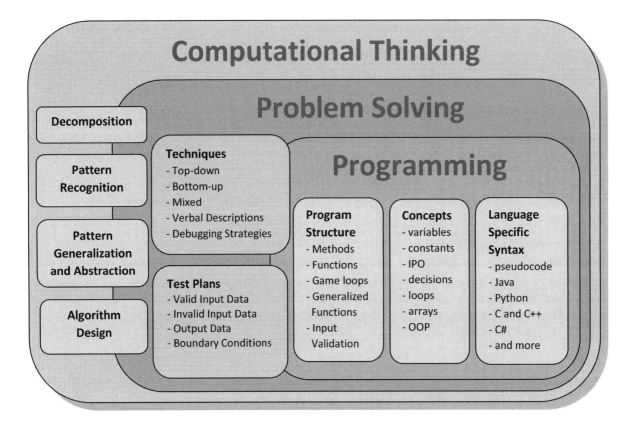

As you can see in the diagram above, programming is a subset of problem-solving, which is a subset of computational thinking. You can't write code to solve a problem if you don't understand the problem or can't imagine a potential solution.

Let's examine each section:

**Computational Thinking** is the thought processes involved in understanding a problem and expressing its solution in such a way that a human or computer can effectively carry it out. Computational Thinking is learning to think logically and clearly. It is learning to write and read lines of code and imagine what happens when the computer runs that code.

**Decomposition** breaks up a complex problem or the solution into smaller parts that are easier to understand, program, and maintain. Any complex problem will consist of many smaller problems to solve. Students run into trouble when they try to solve problems at the program-level instead of breaking down the problem into smaller, more easily completed mini-problems.

**Patterns** are reusable solutions to commonly occurring problems in software design. This book is full of patterns you can use in your own programs. This is NOT plagiarism!

**Pattern Generalization and Abstraction** is the creation of general concepts from specific instances by abstracting common properties. For example, if you write code that can search a two-dimensional array, then you should be able to write code to search a three or four-dimensional array.

**Algorithms** are a sequence of instructions. Like a recipe for cooking a cake, algorithms tell the computer exactly the steps to take to solve the problem. Clarity is more important than the number of lines of code.

A variety of **Problem-Solving Techniques** are used to approach a problem. Different types of problems require different techniques to solve them. If one is not useful, try another.

**Test plans** force the programmer to think about the problem before starting to code. A good test plan lists the inputs and expected outputs for a program. Documenting test cases before writing code enables the programmer to know what to test when the time comes.

**Program Structure** provides useful and solid methods to code a variety of programming tasks. This is the secret of great programmers—they don't reinvent the wheel for every program, they have an encyclopedic memory and library of useful and solid program structures they can use whenever they need to. Rookie programmers resist learning and using existing structures to their own detriment.

There are always new **concepts** to learn no matter how experienced you are. In the beginning, you will learn basic concepts that are applicable to every programming language. Every programming language uses variables, constants, loops, decision-structures, and arrays or something similar.

This book does not show you **language-specific syntax**—it uses pseudocode to be language independent. If you are learning Java, Python, C#, or C++ you should have no problem translating the pseudocode in this book to those languages. If you do have trouble, it means you don't really understand the concepts or the language's syntax.

A Mental Exercise:

Without looking, name the 4 parts of Computational Thinking and describe what they are.

So, what's the take-away from this diagram? That an introductory class in Programming and Problem Solving is more about learning to think than it is learning to code. Students who embrace this do well in the class. Students who just want to learn to code without thinking too hard will have trouble completing their assignments.

Which type of student are you?

## Detail Orientation

Computer scientists must be very detail-oriented. They must be able to look at a program and find the one character that is not right. Here is an example.

Are these two lines of code the same?

for (int x = 0; x <= LEN; x++)                    for (int x = 0; x <= LEN; x++);

They are not the same. How about these two lines?

for (int x = 0; x <= LEN, x++)                    for (int x = 0; x <= LEN; x++)

They are not the same either and not finding the error will result in your program not working. This is the level of detail you need to have to write code. The computer will tell you when you have a some errors, but you still must find the exact error by reading the code line-by-line and character-by-character.

Now you know EVERY character matters. A missing period or semi-colon will cause an error YOU have to find. The good news is that once you know what to look for, it isn't difficult to find the error. But you have to want to and you have to think about what the error message says. The computer will not do your work for you.

The good news is that once you get the hang of it, finding errors becomes easier and easier.

## Some Ideas to Remember

Successful students are not smarter than other students. Successful students just have different skills, habits, and strategies because they see school as a learning process, and not as a place to earn grades.

The idea that demanding work can be satisfying and enjoyable may sound weird to you, but if you look at the activities you enjoy most, you'll see that those are probably the activities at which you work the hardest.

Feeling confused and frustrated is a natural part of learning. If you aren't a little frustrated, then you're not pushing yourself enough.

When given something the teacher says you must know, believe them!

Learning takes time. If you give it time and the proper effort, you will learn it. Start early enough and don't give up!

## Review Questions

You should be able to answer these questions and discuss their meaning. Pretend you are in a job interview—you better know the answers, right?

1.    What is Computational Thinking?
2.    What is Decomposition?
3.    What are Patterns?
4.    What is Pattern Generalization?
5.    What are algorithms?
6.    What is a test plan?

# Chapter 3
# Solving Problems

This chapter presents information on thinking about and solving problems. To truly understand this information, after you have finished reading each chapter in this book, return to this chapter and review the information again.

> *"If I only had an hour to solve a problem, I'd spend 55 minutes thinking about the problem and 5 minutes thinking about solutions."*
> —Albert Einstein

Computer scientists think the problem through before they write one line of code. Many students experience frustration when they try to write code before they really understand the problem or what form the solution will take. By reading this book you will learn a variety of techniques to better understand problems, how to approach solving them, and how to avoid wasting your time.

> *"If you don't know what you're doing, you don't know when to stop."*
> —Unknown

If you know what you are doing, you won't waste your time when you get off track. You'll be able to quickly bring yourself back from the abyss and continue to make progress in solving the problem.

## Have a Plan to Solve the Problem

This textbook demonstrates general processes to follow when solving problems, but, with experience, you will develop your own methods to solve problems. In the meantime, follow the standard processes described in this textbook.

By following a standard process, you will see that you are making progress as you finish each step in the process and will be confident you will eventually solve the problem. Too many students only consider the big problem and become frustrated when they can't solve the whole problem quickly.

By having a plan that decomposes the problem into smaller tasks, you will see the progress you are making and will not be tempted to give up. Writing a program is not the only step in the problem-solving process. The larger the problem, the more steps you will take to solve it.

Don't become frustrated if you can't solve a problem in ten seconds. Any problem of significance will require you think about and struggle with and grapple with the problem before you come up with a solution.

## Expectations

Your job as a computer science student is not only to solve the stated problem by the deadline, but also to use established problem-solving methods and coding structures to do so.

From a *user-interface* perspective, your programs should:

- tell the user what it does when the program starts,
- ask the user to do things in a logical manner,
- ask the user for information before demanding input,
- tell the user specifically what is wrong when they enter invalid data,
- present the output in a neat and structured way with no spelling or grammar errors,
- tell the user when the program is ending, and
- do what the program is supposed to do.

From an *internal program* perspective, your program should:

- contain your name at the top with a short description of what the program does,
- follow best-practices and use standard program structures,
- use descriptive nouns for naming variables and verbs for naming modules and functions,
- break down the code into appropriately small parts with a minimal amount of code in main or in any module or function,
- have every module and function do one thing and ONLY one thing,
- validate all input, and
- not use any concepts or techniques you have not covered in class yet.

From a problem-solving perspective, your program should solve the stated problem while following any stated restrictions. Restrictions are not random! They exist to guide you into writing better code or to use a new concept.

### KEY CONCEPT:

Sometimes a student will complain about not being able to use an advanced technique they already know.

Do these same students tell their art teacher that instead of creating a painting for a painting assignment, they are going to take a photograph instead? Do these same students tell their writing instructor that they are going to make a movie instead of writing an essay? Restrictions exist for a reason.

If you want to know what your teacher wants from you and your program, the above lists of expectations tells you precisely.

## Your Intent

A common problem-solving error is for students to be stuck for hours trying to solve a problem by writing code instead of thinking about the problem and possible solutions. They refuse to use the problem-solving techniques presented in this book. They think they are saving time by writing code first, but they are actually wasting their time.

> *"It is not enough to be busy….*
> *The question is: What are we busy about?"*
> *—Henry David Thoreau*

If you are stuck for more than five minutes, you need to step away from the problem and ask yourself what you are trying to do. Become very clear on your intent.

> *"If you find yourself in a hole, the first thing to do is to stop digging."*
> *—Will Rogers*

Depending on where you are in the problem-solving process, the answers to the question, "What am I trying to do?" could be something like these:

I need to get input from the user.

I need to validate the input is correct.

I need to make sure the number entered has not already been entered.

I need to indent my program in a standard way.

I need to use a basic gaming loop.

I need to produce the required output.

I need to refactor my code to separate input, processing, and output.

I need to take code out of main and put it in functions.

Grappling with a problem means using a variety of problem-solving techniques such as creating a test plan, creating a hierarchy chart, creating an IPO chart, and breaking down the problem into smaller parts. Ask yourself questions. Look for patterns—have you seen anything like this before?

It is very important for you to see each problem as many smaller problems that you CAN do. As you complete the smaller problems, you will gain confidence you are making progress towards solving the larger problem.

If you are still stuck, then you should ask a tutor or your instructor for guidance. They will not write any code for you, but they will point you in the proper direction to think about the problem.

> *"The formulation of the problem is often more important than its solution, which may*
> *be merely a matter of mathematical or experimental skill."*
> *—Albert Einstein*

## What before How

When analyzing a problem, one of the first steps to take is to think about *what* has to happen to solve the problem. Do not jump right to *how* to solve the problem—you can't solve a problem before you know *what* to do.

When I'm writing a program and I become stuck for more than a few minutes, I stop and ask myself,

*"WHAT am I trying to do here?"*

This is a powerful question, perhaps the most powerful question in this book. If I can't answer that question, then I can't code it. Neither can you.

### KEY CONCEPT:

Ask yourself "**What am I trying to do?**" before asking, "How do I do this?"

You can't write a line of code if you can't say **WHAT** it is supposed to do.
The more detailed your answer, the easier the coding becomes.

## Talk Out Loud

When I assign coding problems in class, I'll ask a student who appears to be stuck what they are trying to do and they may reply, "I don't know." I'll ask them a few questions and by answering out loud, they get unstuck. And yet they waited for me to ask them questions instead of asking themselves the same questions to get unstuck.

Talking to yourself is called the rubber-ducky technique. Many programmers have an actual small, yellow rubber duck on their desks to remind them to talk out loud so they can hear themselves think. By describing the problem out loud, and by describing a solution out loud, the next step in solving the problem becomes clear.

### KEY CONCEPT:

Don't keep it all in your head. Tell someone what the problem is—out loud. When you think you have a solution, tell someone the solution—out loud.

When you are stuck, and don't know what to do next, ask yourself what you are trying to do—out loud.

When you are writing code, if you can't say out loud what you are trying to do, you can't write code to do that.

Many times, I have been in a meeting discussing a problem when someone says, "Stop! That's the answer!" By discussing the problem out loud, and by paying attention to what everyone is saying, we solved the problem without specifically trying to. It's almost like magic.

> *"How do I know what I think, until I hear what I say?"*
> —*E.M. Forster*

## Problem-Solving Techniques

Solving a problem is not a passive process of waiting for your brain to come up with an answer. Solving a problem is an active process of trying one problem-solving technique and then another. Through experience, you will learn what techniques work best for different types of problems.

Here are some problem-solving techniques, in no particular order:

- Make a plan, even if some of the steps are not well defined yet
- Restate the problem
- Divide the problem into smaller pieces (decomposition!)
- Start with what you know so you can make progress (pattern recognition!)
- Start at the top of the program and imagine the necessary control structures
- Start at the bottom of the program with the low-level utility routines
- Start with input validation
- Start with the output, passing it sample data to get the required format correct
- Simplify the problem. What if…. ?
- Look for analogies. Have you seen something like this before?
- Write small test programs and experiment. What if I… ?
- Perform an analysis of what could go wrong with your program and then work to avoid that.

Don't become frustrated. Solving a hard problem is more satisfying than solving an easy problem. Accept the challenge of working hard and learning something new!

> *"There is one thing we can do, and the happiest people are those who do it to the limit of their ability. We can be completely present. We can be all here. We can… give all our attention to the opportunity before us."*
> —*Mark Van Doren*

## Syntax and Logic Errors

Computers cannot do anything without being told what to do by a software program. Computers cannot understand a problem in English or any other language like humans can—they need the problem to be translated into a language they understand.

---

 **KEY CONCEPT:**

The computer is only as intelligent as the person who programmed it and no more. A computer will do any illogical thing you ask it to do if it understands the instructions to do so.

The computer is NOT in charge. The software developer is responsible for ensuring their program is correct and does what it is supposed to do. The computer is merely a tool.

---

When writing a program, you will run into two types of errors: syntax and logic.

With a *syntax error*, you write a line of code, but the computer does not understand it. This can happen because you misspelled a keyword or used incorrect punctuation. These errors will be caught by the compiler or interpreter and will give you an error message describing the problem. Below is an example of a syntax error—the word display is misspelled so the computer won't know what to do with it.

```
Dispaly "This is the output"
```

With a *logic error*, you write a line of code, thinking it will do one thing, but it actually does another. These types of errors are harder to find since the computer will not tell you there is an error. There will not be an error message you can read. The only way to find these types of errors is to pay attention to the output and to test your program thoroughly. Below is an example of a logic error—the program will compile and run successfully so the computer thinks it's great. Only a person can tell there is an error in this line of code.

```
Display "Four plus Five is ", 99
```

Rest assured, if you do not notice a logic error, your instructor or your end-user will. Count on it. Testing is crucial to verify the program did what you expected it to do. There is no way around this. Nobody writes code that does not need to be thoroughly tested.

----------

You may be used to your phone or games telling you what you did wrong. As a programmer, this is not the case—it is your job to make the computer do exactly what you want it to do. YOU are in charge. When your software does something, you decide if what it did is correct or not.

## Testing

Every professional programmer spends a lot of time testing and fixing the code they write. You can't avoid it. We're human and we make mistakes. The key is taking the time to look for mistakes and to be able to recognize mistakes when you see them.

 **KEY CONCEPT:**

Great software developers are great testers. They want to find errors in their code so they can fix them.

> *"Always code as if the guy who ends up maintaining your code will be a violent psychopath who knows where you live."*
>
> —*Martin Golding*

Because testing is such a large part of a software developer's life, you should learn to enjoy it. It's a game whose goal is to try to find as many bugs as possible. Good testers pass the class or get to keep their job. Bad testers fail the class or are fired.

 **KEY CONCEPTS:**

Trying to find your errors before the teacher may be a new concept for you. Many students in high school and even in college turn in poor work and hope the teacher doesn't see the problem or hopes the teacher will let it go without comment.

This is NOT what happens in a programming class. The teacher WILL find your bugs and your program will justifiably fail the assignment.

You must change your attitude and enjoy finding bugs in your programs. Only by testing and finding bugs can you ensure your program is correct. Students fail, and programmers are fired, because they stop testing too soon.

You may have become used to earning partial credit in school. If your English paper is OK, but not great, you can expect a B or maybe a C. If your biology lab is good, but not quite right, you may earn an A-.

A programming class is not like that. A programming class is more like a job outside of school. If you worked at a fast-food restaurant and always undercharged the customer, would you receive partial credit? No, you would be fired. The manager expects you do to the job correctly.

If I were to sell you an app for your phone, but every time it ran it sent angry text messages to all your contacts, you would not be happy. If you downloaded a free app that promised one thing, but did another, or only did it partially, you would not use that app again. That app would fail.

> *"If you don't like to test your code, most likely your teacher won't like it either."*
> —Unknown

If a student or an employee cannot be bothered to test their code, then, for their lack of respect towards their teacher or company, they deserve to fail or be fired. Don't imagine your code is perfect—test it! Try to break it. Good testers want to break their code. Bad programmers do as little testing as possible. Which are you? (Your grade will let you know!)

**KEY CONCEPT:**

Software that does not work is worth $0 in the marketplace and should be worth a zero for the assignment in school. There should be no partial credit for shoddy work. Your software works or it does not.

Fortunately, you can tell if your program works by testing it thoroughly. It's not a mystery.

**Question your Assumptions**

When you test you must know your assumptions and what the expected outcome should be. Look at the below statement. What's wrong with it?

2 + 2 = 5

Did your assumptions lead you to think the 5 should be a 4? What about different assumptions? Aren't the below answers correct also?

2 + 3 = 5
3 + 2 = 5
2 + 2 < 5
2 + 2 = 5 - 1

Be aware of and question your assumptions.

## Debugging

Testing a program, finding errors, and fixing the errors is called *debugging*. When you write a program, you think it is correct—after all, you wrote it and you wrote it to work. Unfortunately, no programmer writes perfect code. None. Zip. Nada. We all have to test our code—a lot.

Here is a random, inefficient approach to debugging that too many beginners use:

**1. Surprise**
I can't BELIEVE the program didn't work perfectly. WTF?!

**2. Disgust**
i.e., computers and software suck!

**3. Try to randomly add code to fix the problem**
Maybe THIS will work. Nope. How about THIS? Nope. Computers suck!

**4. Repeat Steps 1-3**
Until time runs out.

**5. Give Up**
Well, nothing I tried worked, so it just can't be fixed. NOBODY can do this.

Here is a better, more scientific and effective approach to debugging:

**1. Observation**
Observe precisely what the program does or does not do. Saying, "it doesn't work" is not detailed enough!

**2. Form a Hypothesis**
i.e., construct a theory to explain the observed behavior. "I think that..."

**3. Test your Hypothesis**
Devise a test to verify whether your hypothesis is correct or not:

- If your hypothesis is correct, you have either already solved it, or you have identified the problem and are ready to repair the error.

- If your hypothesis is not correct, you need to form another hypothesis—and maybe re-check your observations.

**4. Repeat Steps 1-3**
Repeat the process, learning more about the problem each time until the problem is solved.

Here is an example of the above thinking process:

1. Observe – the output is not being displayed at all.
2. Form a Hypothesis – I think the display statement is not being executed.
3. Test your Hypothesis – I don't even *see* a display statement in my code!

So, you add a display statement and then start at the beginning again and observe what happens when you run the program this time. If adding the display statement solved that problem, then you can proceed to test another aspect of your program.

The idea behind debugging is to get more information so you will understand why the program is not working the way you thought it would. The goal is to keep narrowing the problem down to the specific lines of code that are causing the error.

When you have a problem:

- That means something unexpected has happened.
- Think about what went wrong and why it might have happened that way.
- Try to get more information to help you figure out what went wrong.
- Use Display statements to show the values of variables at critical points in the program.
- Use the debug mode of the IDE to view variables as the program runs.
- Display the values of internal variables—such as counters—as the program runs.
- Be confident that once you have enough information, you will be able to identify the bug, and you will be able to fix it.

## Test Plans

A test plan is a list of all possible types of inputs and the expected outputs for those inputs. Many, if not most employees in a software company do not write code. There are many jobs in software development that focus on creating test plans or use already created test plans for testing code.

Some test plans are very structured and use a spreadsheet to organize the test cases, and some test plans are less structured. Test plans should be written before writing one line of code. You should have already created a test plan when you begin to test your code. You don't want to have to create a test plan late at night when the program is due by midnight. Creating a good test plan takes thought and a fresh mind. The good news is that you will get faster at creating test plans as you create more of them.

> *"Before everything else, getting ready is the key to success."*
> —*Henry Ford*

Why create a test plan?

- To deepen your understanding of the problem
- To reveal data issues that were not apparent in the problem statement
- To focus your thinking on the important input and output aspects of the program

What should be in a test plan?

- All inputs (data being entered by the user, data being read from a file, random input)
  - All types of invalid data
    - Error messages to be displayed when invalid data is encountered
  - All types of valid data
- Expected Outputs (text to the console, a file, sound, fireworks, whatever)
- Combinations of input data that will exercise all parts of the code

Here is an example of a test plan for this small problem:

Ask the user to enter the speed in miles per hour they were traveling. Determine if they were going over 75 mph. If so, display "You were speeding!" If not, display "Have fun!"

| Inputs | Output | Result OK or Not? |
|---|---|---|
| 0 | Have fun! | |
| 75 | Have fun! | |
| 76 | You were speeding! | |
| -55 | Error message: Invalid input | |
| A | Error message: Invalid input | |
| null | Error message: Invalid input | |
| spaces | Error message: Invalid input | |

**Note:** null means the user pressed the enter key without entering anything at all.

A test plan should be easy enough for your grandfather to read and follow. He should know exactly the values to enter and what should happen. He should be able to tell you if the program worked as expected or not.

Having a test plan enables you to test your program without having to create test conditions on the fly. The more complicated the program, the more important a written test plan is to complete the assignment successfully.

Another use of a test plan is to give confidence to your manager and your customers that you have tested your program thoroughly. They will not take your word on something like that. They will want to see the documentation of what values you entered into your program and what happened.

KEY CONCEPTS:

You should also be aware that a completed test plan is like a legal contract. When, as the programmer, you say you have tested your program with these input values and this is what happened, then the user's and your company's management should be able to trust you.

If your customers run the program with the same input values and they receive different output, you will not have a job for long. Let me be clear here: you will be fired for lying to your management. In class, you should receive a zero for the assignment if your test plan is not complete or not correct. Lying to people who are counting on you is never acceptable.

## Boundary Conditions

Many problems have boundary conditions to test for. The better you understand this concept, the faster and more complete your test plans will be. Here is a simple example:

Problem Statement:
The program should ask the user to enter a whole number greater than 10.

Possible types of invalid input values: (yes, you have to test for these too!)

A, &, space, null, 3.1415

Possible valid input values and a comment about each one:

| Input value | Comment | Expected Output |
| --- | --- | --- |
| -1 | Always test a negative number | Error message |
| 0 | Always test for 0 | Error message |
| 9 | One less than the stated number in the problem (10) | Error message |
| 10 | The number stated in the problem | OK |
| 11 | One more than the number stated in the problem (10) | OK |

Do you think you need to test for more values? Probably not. If the program works correctly for -1, displaying an error message, then it should work for -2, -3, -4, etc. If the program works for 11, then it should work for 12, 13, 14, etc. Just to be sure you might want to test two input values such as -9999 and 3333 to give yourself confidence the program works for all values in those ranges.

The goal is to test as much as you should, but no more. After all, you're a busy person, right?

## Are You Stuck?

Being stuck is normal. Computational problems can be difficult. Continue to use the problem-solving techniques in this book and gathered through experience to make progress in your understanding. If you are stuck, it's probably because you don't understand the problem well enough to imagine a solution.

What do you do when you don't know what to do?

- Try to understand the problem by describing it in your own words to someone else.
- Write a test plan that identifies the possible inputs and expected outputs for each input.
- Break down complicated areas into smaller and smaller tasks.
- Create a Hierarchy Chart of modules and functions (after we have covered modules and functions in Chapter 5).
- Describe out loud what a possible solution might look like. What kind of control structures do you think the solution might need? What kind of input validation?
- Refer to *Appendix B: Problem-Solving Roadmap* as a structured method to solving first-semester software problems.

## Review Questions

You should be able to answer these questions, discuss their meaning, and give an example. Pretend you are in a job interview—you should know the answers, right?

1. What is the most powerful question to ask when trying to solve a programming problem?

2. Name five problem-solving techniques.

3. What is a syntax error? Give an example.

4. What is a logic error? Give an example.

5. What is debugging?

6. Name the four steps of the Scientific method for debugging a software program.

7. Why do programmers create test plans?

8. What should a test plan consist of?

9. What are boundary conditions? Give an example.

10. From a user-interface perspective, what should your program do?

11. From an internal program perspective, what should your program do?

12. What should you do when you don't know what to do next?

*There is no expedient to which a person will not go to avoid the real labor of thinking.*
                              —*Thomas Edison (paraphrased)*

*Are you willing to leave your comfort zone?*

I'm having an identity crisis!

Me too!

# Chapter 4
# Variables and Constants

What is a software program? It's a set of sequential instructions that tells the computer what to do. Since computers don't understand English, Spanish, Chinese, or any other human language, you must write the program in a language the computer understands.

In this book, we use pseudocode to be platform-independent. That means you should be able to take the concepts you learn here and write a computer program in the software language of your choice with the help of a language-specific textbook or reference book. This book will cover basic coding concepts so you can write good code in Java, Python, C, C++, C#, or most any other software language.

## Terminology You must Know

The first step to learning a computer language is to learn the words used in that language and what they mean. Each chapter will list the words from that chapter you need to be able to define and describe out loud. If you can't define a word out loud, you don't know it! Here is the list for this chapter:

| | | | | |
|---|---|---|---|---|
| Pseudocode | Program | Input | Algorithm | Real variable type |
| Constant | UpperCase | Processing | Integer | String variable type |
| Variable | CamelCase | Output | Real numbers | Integer variable type |
| Prompt | Display | Strings | String Literals | Numeric literal |

## Sample Pseudocode

Each chapter will introduce a new set of pseudocode statements that a computer will understand. In this chapter statements like the following will be introduced. By the end of the chapter, you must be able to read and write each of these lines of code before you move onto the next chapter.

```
//Lines starting "//" are comments and not executed by the computer
Declare Constant String GREETING = "Hello, "
Declare String username
Display "Enter your name"
Input userName
Display GREETING, userName, ". Welcome!"
```

Output from the small program above:
```
Enter your name
Bob                        <-- the user typed this
Hello, Bob. Welcome!
```

## Variables and Constants

Almost all software programs use variables and constants. Variables and constants hold values for the program. For example, a variable named *playerHealthAmount* may hold values from 0 to 100 and be initialized to 100 when the program starts.

**Variables** vary as the program runs. The values a variable holds will change over time. Many languages, including the pseudocode in this book, require the programmer to declare the type of data the variable contains before the variable is used. For variable types in this book, we will use *String*, *Integer*, *Real*, and *Boolean*. Real numbers contain decimals. Variables are named using the *camelCase* standard: the descriptive words are put together with the first letter capitalized likeThis.

**Constants** are constant and their value does not change as the program runs. They stay the same FOREVER. (Well, as long as the program runs). Constants are named in UPPER_CASE. Constants also must be declared to be a type of variable and set to a value.

Examples:

```
//Variables - anything after // is ignored by the computer.
Declare Integer age
Declare String name
Declare Real Salary

//Constants - this line is a comment that the computer ignores.
Declare Constant Integer FIRST_LEVEL = 21
Declare Constant String NAME = "Bob"
```

Notice that constants must be declared and initialized on the same line. That's possible for variables also:

```
Declare String name = "Not entered yet"
```

## Naming Standards

Variables and Constants hold data. They are named with **nouns** that describe what they hold.

**KEY CONCEPTS:**

**Variables** in many programming languages are named using the **camelCase** naming standard. That is what we use in this textbook.

**Constants** are named using **UPPER_CASE**.

Note that the computer doesn't care about naming standards—they are for us humans to use so we can read the code easier.

If your company or another instructor has a different standard, just follow their guidance. It's not a big deal to conform to the desired naming standard—you will get used to it very quickly.

With a few exceptions you will learn about later, variable names should describe the data the variable holds. They should be self-explanatory.

Bad variable names make the code harder to write and harder to read. In the left column below are examples of bad variable and constant names. Can you tell what values the variables and constants in the left column hold? Look at the variable and constant names in the right column. Can you tell what values they hold?

| Bad variable names: | Good variable names: |
|---|---|
| num | numberOfMonths |
| aNumber | numberToProcess |
| totalE | totalEmployees |
| stuff | temporaryValue |
| pct | percentFailure |
| tPctB4calcs | totalPercentBeforeCalcs |
| aRandoNum | randomNumber |

| Bad constant names: | Good constant names: |
|---|---|
| daysInWeek | DAYS_IN_WEEK |
| STATETAX | STATE_TAX_PERCENT |
| County_Tax | COUNTY_TAX_AMOUNT |
| F_TAX | FEDERAL_TAX_AMOUNT |
| p_amt | PAYROLL_AMT |
| #_EMPLOYEES | NBR_OF_EMPLOYEES |
| MAX-HIT-POINTS | MAX_HIT_POINTS |

 **KEY CONCEPT:**

Variables and constants should be named for what information they hold.

You should be able to ask your grandmother what a variable holds and she could tell you from reading the name.

A *numeric literal* is a number such as -1, 0, 3.1415, and 102.

A *String literal* is text defined in quotes like this: "Test".

## Declaring Variables and Constants

Variables and constants can hold all types of data such as Integers, Strings, and Real numbers. Here are some examples:

**Integer** – whole numbers such as -1, 0, 1, 2, 3, 11, 46, 101, etc.

**Real** – decimal numbers such as 3.0, 3.1415, 10.99, .02, 1.10, 77.0, 101.0, etc.

**String** – text such as "Bob", "5", "Total=", "SUMMARY", "Sale Price:"

In many programing languages, Variables and Constants must be declared before they are used so the computer knows what type they are and can allocate enough space in memory to hold the value.

This book uses the convention where variables must be declared a type and their type cannot change—this is called *strongly-typed*. Other software languages are *loosely-typed* which means you don't have to declare the type of variable before using it and the program may change its type as the program runs.

Examples of declaring variables and constants in pseudocode:

```
Declare Integer myCounter = 0

Declare String employeeName = "default name"

Declare Real costOfCar = 23999.99

Declare Constant Real SALES_TAX = .02    //represents 2%
```

## Displaying Output

To show the user of your program some text on the screen, use the *Display* statement.

```
Display "Hello Brave New World!"
Display "Goodbye Cruel World!"
```

The above lines will show the below text when the program runs:

```
Hello Brave New World!
Goodbye Cruel World!
```

Any time you want to display text, numbers, or symbols to the user, use the *Display* statement. Display lines can be broken up into pieces, such as when there is not enough room on the screen to show everything.

Note that in a *Display* statement you can display more than one piece of data by separating them with a comma ( , ). This will be done differently in different programming languages, but don't worry about that. When the time comes this kind of translation from pseudocode to a specific programming language will be easy.

Examples:

```
Display "Hello ", "Brave ", "New ", "World!"

Display "Goodbye ",
        "Cruel World!"

Display "This " + " concatenates " + "strings!"
```

Note that the word *Display* is a reserved word in pseudocode and you can't use it for anything else. To write a display statement in Java or Python, refer to *Appendix H: Pseudocode to Java Examples* and *Appendix I: Pseudocode to Python Examples* to view examples of converting Pseudocode to those languages.

### Truncating Real Numbers

Integers are round numbers. If you set an integer to a Real number, the decimal portion of the number is discarded. This comes in handy in programming so it is something to be aware of.

```
Declare Real piValue = 3.1415
Declare Integer integerPiValue = piValue
Display "integerPiValue is ", integerPiValue
```

Results in this:
```
integerPiValue is 3
```

The variable's value is now 3 because the .1415 portion of the number was truncated.

## Getting Input

Displaying text is great, but most programs will need to ask the user to enter some data. To do that, use a *prompt*. A prompt is a question or statement displayed to the user on the screen telling them what to do.

Use the *Input* pseudocode statement with a variable to get the entered value from the user as shown below. The input statement uses a variable that must be declared before it is used. Here is a short program that demonstrates how to use *Display* and *Input* statements:

```
Main
      Declare String userName
      Display "Please enter your name"
      Input userName
      Display "Your name is ", userName
End Main
```

Can you tell someone what each line does? If not, go back and re-read this chapter from the beginning again. Don't fall behind because you don't understand!

Here is the output from the small program above:

```
Please enter your name
Bob                        <-- the user typed this
Your name is Bob
```

When asking for input, always *prompt* the user and tell them what you are asking for, as in this code-snippet:

```
Declare String newValue
Display "Please enter a word"
Input newValue
//other code not shown
```

An *Input* statement will almost always be paired up with a *Display* statement so the user knows what to enter.

## Formulas

Formulas are mathematical expressions that do calculations and put the result in a variable. The variable is on the left of the equals sign and the formula is on the right. In formulas such as this:

```
newValue = 4 + 5
```

The calculated value on the right of the equal sign is stored in the memory location of the variable on the left of the equal sign. After the above formula is executed, the value of the variable *newValue* is 9.

In formulas, the arithmetic operators are executed in the order shown below, from left to right:

|  |  |
|---|---|
| ( ) | parentheses |
| ^ | exponents |
| * / MOD | multiplication, division, and modulus |
| + - | addition and subtraction |

Formulas like the below are called processing statements. They don't get input, and they don't display output. They process data. Here are some more examples:

```
newSalary = oldSalary + oldSalary * raisePercent
age = age + 1
force = gravity * ((mass1 * mass2) / distance^2)
```

In this example, the exponent is done first, and then the multiplication:

```
energy = mass * (speedOfLight)^2
```

### Incrementing and Decrementing

Two common formula operators you must know are ++ and --. The below two lines of code, that increments the variable *counter*, do the exact same thing:

```
counter = counter + 1
counter++
```

The ++ is a shortcut and saves time in typing and reading the code. So, what do you think this line of code does?

```
counter--
```

That's right. It subtracts one from the value of the variable named counter (decrementing). You have recognized a pattern and generalized it to arrive at the answer using computational thinking! Well done!

### Integer Division

Remember that Integers truncate Real numbers? The same thing happens when two Integers are divided:

```
Declare Real x = 3 / 2
Display "x is ", x
```

That code displays the below text, despite the variable x being a Real number:

```
x is 1
```

Why? Because the result of the division is 1.5, but the decimal portion of the number is discarded because the result of two integers being divided is an integer. To avoid that result, tell the computer to keep the decimals:

```
Declare Real x = 3 / 2.0
```

An Integer divided by a Real number is a Real number!

## Input, Processing, and Output

A well-structured program separates the *input* code from the *processing* code and from the *output* code. Input comes first, then processing, and then output. Every program will have input and output.

Let's try reading a simple problem and identify the Inputs, the Processing, and the Outputs (IPO):

> This is a special multiplication program for zoos. This program will ask the zookeeper to enter two numbers, multiply the two numbers, and then produce a report to show all the numbers used in the program.

What is the most important part of the problem? The bold parts below.

> This is a special multiplication program for zoos. This program will ask the zookeeper to **enter two numbers**, **multiply the two numbers**, and then produce a report to **show all the numbers** used in the program.

Note that the problem may not be worded in the sequence the program will run. You may have to reorganize the problem:

> This is a special multiplication program for zoos. This program will **report all numbers** used in the process. The program will **multiply two numbers entered** by the zookeeper.

Despite how the problem is stated, the final program will always follow the IPO structure.

```
Main
        Declare Real firstNbr, secondNbr, total

        //Input statements
        Display "Enter the first number to multiply"
        Input firstNbr

        Display "Enter the second number to multiply"
        Input secondNbr

        //Processing statement
        total = firstNbr * secondNbr

        //Output statement
        Display firstNbr, " * ", secondNbr, " equals ",  total

End Main
```

## How to Write a Program

There are many ways to write a program, but we are going to start simply. As an example and a model to follow, let's create a small program to demonstrate IPO. Read the following problem statement:

> Create a receipt for the customer. Ask the cashier to enter the name of the item being purchased, the number of items being purchased, and the cost of the item. Then calculate the total cost and display all four pieces of information to the customer.

First, analyze (think about) **what** needs to be done. The problem statement tells you directly!

Then, design **how** you will do that in a software program. As you gain experience you will have more design tools to help you with the design.

A good first step is to write down your thoughts in comments. Think about WHAT has to happen, not HOW it will be coded. We will use "//" to identify comments in the program.  Comments are lines of code that are informational only and are not executed by the computer.

```
Main
      //Declare variables and constants for this program
      //Input: Get input from the customer
      //Processing: Calculate the total cost
      //Output: Display the receipt to the customer
End Main
```

Notice that the above program is in IPO order already! Now, let's fill out more details from the problem statement...

```
Main
      //Declare variables and constants for this program
      //     Declare name of the item
      //     Declare the number of items purchased
      //     Declare the price of the item
      //Input: Get input from the customer:
      //     get the name of item
      //     get the number of items purchased
      //     get the price of item
      //Processing: Calculate the total cost
      //     multiply the number of items purchased
      //          by the price of the item
      //Output: Display the receipt to the customer:
      //     Display the name of item
      //     Display the number of items purchased
      //     Display the price of the item
      //     Display the total cost
End Main
```

Notice that in the above program you haven't written any code yet, but the program is almost complete. Yes, programming feels like magic when you approach it the right way!

Now, let's convert each line into code. This is the easy part of programming. The hard part is knowing what to code, but you have already done that work above!

Let's look at the actual program (compare the below code to the program on the previous page):

```
Main

        //Declare variables and constants for this program
        Declare String   nameOfItem
        Declare Integer  numberOfItemsPurchased
        Declare Real     priceOfItem

        //Get input from the customer
        Display "What are you purchasing?"
        Input nameOfItem
        Display "Please enter the number of items bought"
        Input numberOfItemsPurchased
        Display "Please enter the price of the item"
        Input priceOfItem

        //Calculate the total cost
        Declare Real totalCost
        totalCost = numberOfItemsPurchased * priceOfItem

        //Display the receipt to the customer
        Display "------ Receipt ------"
        Display "Item Purchased:      ", nameOfItem
        Display "Number purchased:    ", numberOfItemsPurchased
        Display "Price of Each Item: ", priceOfItem
        Display "Total Cost:          ", totalCost
End Main
```

Here are some things to notice about this program:

- The program is structured with IPO principles. Input comes before processing and only then does output happen.
- Notice that the *totalCost* is Declared in the processing section. We did that because it is used in the processing section. But it is also acceptable to move the *Declare Real totalCost* line to the top of the program or module.
- The names of the variables are consistent throughout the program.

A Mental Exercise:

Identify everywhere the variable *priceOfItem* is used in the program. Is it Declared, Input, Processed, and then Output? How about *totalCost*?

What would you do if a variable has not been Declared? Or it is input, but not used afterward?

These are the kind of questions you should ask yourself when reviewing your programs.

Sometimes an error does not cause the program to crash or to run incorrectly—it's just freaking annoying for anyone reading the code. Look at how this code is formatted and indented:

```
                          Main
      //Declare variables and constants needed for this program
      Declare String   nameOfItem
            Declare Integer         numberOfItemsPurchased
        Declare Real     priceOfItem


   //  Get input         from the          customer
            Display "What are you purchasing?"
              Input
                   nameOfItem
            Display "Please enter the number of items bought"
                    Input       numberOfItemsPurchased
       Display        "Please enter the cost of the item"
         Input                       priceOfItem


                   //Calculate        the       total cost
            Declare Real totalCost
               totalCost = numberOfItemsPurchased * priceOfItem


            //    Display the receipt to         the customer
       Display        "------ Receipt ------"
          Display      "Item Purchased:       ",       nameOfItem
        Display
                           "Number purchased:    ",
           numberOfItemsPurchased
             Display "Price of Each Item: ", priceOfItem
        Display        "Total Cost:            ", totalCost
                      End Main
```

This is the same program as shown on the previous page. Is the code on this page easy to read? No. Was it easy to write? Doubt it. Can it be maintained? Not easily. If you insist on writing code like this in your job, you will quickly become unemployed!

**KEY CONCEPT:**
Programs MUST be indented in a standard manner. Proper indentions make the code easier to write, easier to read, and easier to debug. Get in the habit of indenting your code correctly!

## Programming and Problem Solving

Writing a bug-free program is not easy, but it can be done. People do it all the time but only after fixing all the bugs they found during testing their program. After you create a program, or while you are writing it, ask yourself questions about your code. Only by examining your code using a structured method will you find the bugs you created.

Some questions to ask yourself include:

- Are all the variables declared using the camelCase naming standard?
- Are all variables used?
- Are constants declared using the UPPER_CASE naming standard?
- Are constants declared and initialized in the same line?
- Are all constants used?
- Do variable and constant names accurately describe the values they hold?
- Does every *Input* statement have a *Display* statement before it?
- Does the program follow the IPO structure?
- Does the output look *exactly* like the required output?
- Have I documented each section of the code?

If you follow best practices, follow IPO principles, read the textbook, ask questions, and practice writing code outside of your assignments, then you will have a very good chance of writing good, bug-free code.

--------------------

If you are wondering about what the teacher wants from your programs,

- Refer to the list of **qualities of good code** on page 21.
- Refer to the list of **expectations for the user-interface** on page 26.
- Refer to the list of **internal program expectations** on page 26.
- Refer to *Appendix C: Testplan Checklist* and to *Appendix D: Program Checklist* for a structured method of reviewing your program's code.

*"Whether you think you can, or you think you can't—you're right."*

*—Henry Ford*

*You can write good code if you think before you act!*

## Design and then Code

Programs must be designed before they are coded. If you try to write code before thinking through the problem, you have to think through the problem AT THE SAME TIME you are trying to write code. This makes writing code more difficult than it has to be. Don't fall into that trap!

The larger and more complicated the program, the more thinking and design work you will do before starting to write code.

**DANGER!**

This is a point where students try to cut corners and end up costing themselves time and effort. There are places to cut corners in programming once you know the basics, but your FIRST programming class is not the place to do that. Following a defined process will help you save time until you have enough experience to know where you can take shortcuts.

How will you know if you fell into this trap of cutting corners?

You may successfully cut corners for the first few easy, small programs. But, as soon as you hit a more difficult program, you will become frustrated and spend A LOT of time trying to write code that could have been done easily if you had only thought about it first. Or you may give up and withdraw from the course—all because you refused to follow the process programmers have been using for decades to design and write programs.

But you're special, right? Sorry, but nobody besides you and your parents think that. You are like every other student learning computer science. The choices and decisions you make when analyzing a problem will determine how easy it is for you to code the solution.

**DANGER!**

"I got it to work! But I don't understand why it works."

Then you are not done. You were probably trying this and trying that and hoping something would work. This is a very inefficient method of problem solving and not repeatable.

You should write code with clear intent. You should know what each line of code is supposed to do. If you don't, then you don't understand the concepts well enough yet.

## Review Questions

You should be able to answer these questions, discuss their meaning, and give an example. Pretend you are in a job interview—you should know the answers, right?

1. What is pseudocode?

2. What is a variable?

3. What is a constant?

4. How are variables and constants named?

5. What is the naming standard for variables?

6. What is the naming standard for constants?

7. Name three data types.

8. What pseudocode statement puts text on the screen?

9. What pseudocode statement gets data from the user?

10. What is a prompt?

11. In what order are arithmetic operators executed?

12. What is the meaning of this: `x++`    and this: `counter--`

13. What does IPO stand for?

14. Does indenting your code matter? Is it important to follow standards?

15. List five very specific questions you could ask about any program to help you find errors.

> Now is a good time to go back and review *Chapter 3: Solving Problems*. The testing and debugging strategies discussed in that chapter will make more sense to you now.

## Can You Do This?

Can you do answer the questions in the prior section, and can you do the below exercises? If not, read this chapter again, go to tutoring, and ask questions in class. You will not be a successful software developer without understanding EVERYTHING in this chapter.

Thousands of students learn this material every semester which means you can too!

Exercises:

1.  Write a short program in pseudocode to ask the user for their name, and then display their name:

    ```
    What is your Name? David
    Your name is David
    ```

2.  Write a short program in pseudocode to ask the user for the number of coffee and muffins they are purchasing. The price of a cup of coffee is $5 and the price of a muffin is $4. Calculate 6% tax on the subtotal. Display a receipt formatted EXACTLY like the below example (as best you can in pseudocode):

    ```
    ****************************************
            My Coffee and Muffin Shop

    Number of coffees bought? 1
    Number of muffins bought? 2

    ****************************************
    ```

    > The user entered 1 and 2 with their keyboard.

    ```
    ****************************************
        My Coffee and Muffin Shop Receipt

    1 Coffee  at $5 each:      $   5.00
    2 Muffins at $4 each:      $   8.00
        6% tax:                $    .78
                               ---------
    Total:                     $  13.78
    ****************************************
    ```

    Would your program's output look exactly like the above? Are the number of * exactly the same as shown in the sample output above? (there are 39 of them) If not, you get NO credit for the assignment (your customer will not pay you if you were doing this for money). Details matter!

# Chapter 5
# Modules and Functions

Modules and functions are lines of code that are *called* from another part of the program or from another program altogether. After the lines of code in the module are executed by the computer, control returns to the *calling statement* (the statement that called the module).

The below diagram shows the order the statements are executed (1,2,3, etc.):

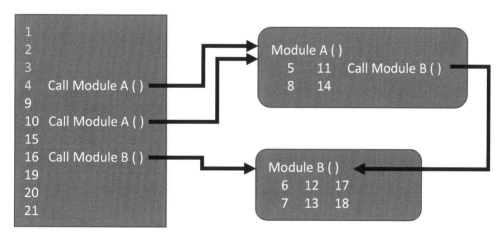

Notice that Module A is used twice and Module B was called by the main program and by Module A! After a module is executed, control returns to the calling statement and the program continues to execute line-by-line.

## Terminology You must Know

You need to be able to define and describe the below words out loud. If you can't define the below words out loud, you don't know them! Software is a language, so you have to learn the terminology.

| | | | |
|---|---|---|---|
| Module | Module header | Return variable type | IPO Chart |
| Function | Function header | Calling statement | Pass by value |
| Parameters | Return | Local variable | Pass by reference |
| Arguments | Scope | Hierarchy Chart | Global constant |

## Sample Pseudocode

By the end of this chapter, you must be able to read and write each of these lines of code before you move on.

```
Module displayHello()          //passing no arguments
Module displayName(name)       //passing one argument


Function Integer getAge()       //Returns an Integer
Function String getName(message) //One parameter, Returns a String

Return name                    //Returns the value of name
Return (age + 10)              //Returns a value
```

## Modules

Modules and functions are the backbones of all programs of any size. Remember the first part of Computational Thinking? Decomposition: breaking down problems into smaller parts. Modules and functions allow programmers to break down large programs into smaller parts.

Why use modules and functions?

- Smaller chunks of code are easier to write, read, debug, and modify
- They can be reused in your program or by other programs
- Writing many smaller pieces of code is faster than writing one big piece of code
- Multiple people can work on different parts of the program at the same time

Modules and function can call other modules and functions. There is no limit you have to worry about!

**Important!** Variables and constants declared in a module are only known in that module. This is called *local scope*. If you want to make a constant known to the entire program, it must be declared globally like this above main:

```
Declare Global Constant String JANUARY = "January"
Main
        //the program continues…
End Main
```

Here is an example of how Modules are called and defined:

```
Main
        displayHello()     //Calls the module to execute its code
End Main

Module displayHello ()  //This is the module header
        Display "Hello!"
End Module
```

## Arguments and Parameters

Data can be passed to modules, or not. In the prior example, the parameter list was empty. The parameter list goes in the ( ) if any values were being passed to the module header from the calling statement. A parameter list is a list of values that are being passed to the module or function.

The *calling statement* sends the values, called *arguments*, to the module or function, where the values are called *parameters*. (Don't ask. Call them both parameters in casual conversation and programmers will know what you mean.)

Here is an example of values being sent to a module instead of being displayed in main:

```
Main

    Declare Constant String SCHOOL_NAME = "State University"
    Declare String username

    Display "Please enter your name"
    Input username

    displayOutput (userName, SCHOOL_NAME, 2020)
End Main
```

and here is the module:

```
Module displayOutput (String uName,
                      String sName,
                      Integer year)
    Display uName,
            ", is enrolled in ", sName,
            " in ", year,
            "."
End Module
```

Here is what is displayed by the above code if the user entered "David" as the user name:

```
David is enrolled in State University in 2020.
```

There are a few things to notice about this example.

1.  The variables in the calling statement are in the same order as the variables in the module header. The computer moves the variables first-to-first, second-to-second, etc...). The argument list and the parameter list MUST be in the same order or the program may crash.

2.  The variable *userName* is declared in main and passed to the module *displayOutput*, but it is renamed in the module to *uName*. That is because only the value is being passed and the variable name can be named anything you want to name it. The computer does not care. To prevent confusing the two and perhaps wasting time during testing and debugging, it is good practice to change the variable names in the calling statement and the module or function header.

3.    The argument list in the calling statement is a list of variables. The variables in the argument list have already been declared in the scope of the calling statement. The parameter list in the module header contains the variable type in addition to variable names. The variables in the module header are new to the module so the computer must be told what kind of variables they are.

4.    The list of arguments and the list of parameters can span multiple lines. Sometimes a long list of variables just won't fit on one line.

5.    A constant, SCHOOL_NAME is sent to the module, but it is received as the variable, sName. The constant in Main is not a constant in the module.

6.    The *Display* statement in the module has divided up the statement into multiple lines to make it easier to read and understand at a glance.

## Functions

The main difference between modules and functions is that a function returns a value to the calling statement and the function header contains the *variable type* of the data being returned. Here is a sample program showing how a function is called and how it returns a value to the calling statement.

```
Main
      Declare String userName
      userName = getInputValue ("Please enter your name")
      displayOutput (userName)
End Main

Function String getInputValue (String message)  //The Function Header
      Declare String uName

      Display message
      Input uName

      Return uName
End Function
```

The same rules apply to functions as apply to modules: the list of arguments must be in the same order as the list of parameters, etc. But now there is new functionality to understand:

1.    The function header contains the *return variable type* of the variable that is being returned. In the above example, the function returns a String.
2.    The function requires a *Return* statement to send a value back to the calling statement.
3.    Note that after the return statement, control returns to the calling statement and the returned value is used.

Make sure that every returned value is used afterward. If it is not being used, don't return a value at all and make it a module instead.

## Naming Standards

Remember that variables and constants are memory locations that hold information so they are named with descriptive **nouns** such as:

firstName, employeeNumber, schoolName, totalAmount, MonsterHealth

Modules and Function names follow the same *camelCase* naming standard as variables, but they are named with **verbs** since they **DO** something. You know it is a module or a function when there is () after the name.

Here are some good module names with the verb in bold so you can easily see the verb:

**display**ProgramInformation()
**display**OutputReport()
**show**UserDashboard (uName)

Here are some good function names with the verb in bold so you can easily see the verb. Notice the verbs suggest a value is being returned from the function.

**get**EmployeeSalary()
**get**PlayerName()
**determine**NewHealthValue()
**calculate**TotalHealth()

If you asked your grandfather what any of the above modules or functions do, he should be able to read the name of the module and know exactly what it does.

By naming your variables, constants, modules, and functions descriptively, you will be able to code, test, and debug your program much easier than if you name them poorly. If you don't know what to name a module, just answer this question out loud:

"What does this module DO?"

You should be able to read your program like it is English. Naming modules and variables appropriately is especially important to make your life easier!

**KEY CONCEPTS:**
- Modules and functions **DO** something, so they should be named using **verbs**.
- A function is just a module that returns a value.  A module does NOT return a value.
- The *return variable type* in the function header tells the computer the type of variable that is being returned: Integer, Real, String, or Boolean.

## Contents of a Module or Function

I hope you noticed module and function names describe what the module or function does. There is nothing secret in the module or function—the name tells you what it does. This brings us to a key concept:

> **KEY CONCEPT:**
> A module or a function should do ONE thing and ONE thing only!

By naming your modules for what they do, you can tell if you are following this key concept or not. For example, below are two BAD module names, and therefore the modules are doing too much.

```
calculateTotalAndDisplayOutput()

getInputDoCalculationsAndDisplayOutput()
```

Wow! That last one is terrible because it does Input, Processing, and Output (IPO)! If you must use the word "and" in describing what module does, then the module does too much. The last module could have been broken up (decomposed!) into the following code snippet:

```
Declare Integer age
age = getInput ()                 //input

result = doCalculations (age)     //processing

displayOutput (result)            //output
```

The above code now follows the standard IPO structure.

Students sometimes write a module that does both calculations and output and then just name it *doCalculations*, or just *displayAnswer*. In naming the module they ignore what the module really does and hopes the teacher or employer doesn't notice. Good luck with that. We're looking for that in your code!

Now that you can write modules, don't forget the principle of IPO. You will write input functions, processing functions, and output modules. They should be separate from each other! Do not combine Input code with Processing code, or Processing code with Output code, or, heaven forbid, I with P and O.

## Scope

*Scope* refers to where a variable or constant is declared and is known to the program. Each module is its own little program and only knows about the variables declared in the module or is defined in the parameter list in the module header. A variable declared in a module or function is called a *local* variable. A *local* variable can only be used in the module or function where it was declared.

A constant declared in a module or function is called a *local* constant. A *local* constant can only be used in the module or function where it was declared.

Below is an example of bad code. Can you see what is wrong?

```
Main

        Declare String userName = "Bob"
        displayWelcome ( )

End Main

Module displayWelcome ( )
        Display "Welcome, ", userName
End Module
```

In the above code, the module *displayWelcome()* does not "know" about the variable *userName* since *userName* was declared in Main and is not declared in the module. To fix this, we pass the value of the variable to the module like this:

```
Main

        Declare String userName = "Bob"
        displayWelcome (userName)          //pass the value

End Main

Module displayWelcome (String uName ) //receive the value
        Display "Welcome, ", uName
End Module
```

**KEY CONCEPTS:**
- Variables should be declared in the section of code they are used in.
- A local variable can only be used in the module or function where it was declared.
- A local variable can only be declared once in a module or function.
- Global constants can be declared at the top of the program.
- Never use global variables unless they have been approved by your teacher or company's system architect.

## Common Mistakes

There are several common mistakes beginners make with modules and functions.

What is wrong with the below code?

```
Declare String message
Declare Integer age
message = "Please enter your age."
age = getAge(String message)
```

It is incorrect for the function call to include the variable type *String*. Note the variable *message* has already been declared as a String in the program. The computer doesn't need it to be defined again. The student has confused the calling statement with the module header.

---

Here is another common mistake in a module or function header:

```
Module getAge(myVariable)
        //some code
End Module
```

Note that the variable type for the incoming parameter *myVariable* is not defined. Is it a String or an Integer? The computer won't know what kind of variable it is unless you tell it.

So, in the first example, the student defined the type of variable twice, and in the second example, the student didn't declare the type of variable at all. Again, you don't have to memorize this if you understand the computer must know what kind of variable it is at all times and you have to tell it!

The header line for the above module should have looked like this:

```
Module getAge(String myVariable)
```

---

Another common mistake is to pass an argument to a module that should be declared in the module itself. For example:

```
Declare Integer age = 0
age = getAge("Enter your age", age)
```

Notice that the variable *age* in the above line is ALWAYS 0. So why pass it at all? You shouldn't.

Here is the code, corrected:

```
Declare Integer age = 0
age = getAge("Enter your age")
```

**KEY CONCEPT:**

The argument being sent when the module is called, and the receiving parameter variable in the module header, must be of the same data type.

If there is more than 1 argument-parameter, they must be in the same order in the calling statement and in the module header.

Here is another common Error. Notice the argument list is different from the parameter list so this code will cause an error.

```
Main
      Declare Integer num, dNum
      Display "Enter a number"
      Input num
      dNum = doubleNumber (num, "Doubling…")   //Integer, String
      Display "2 x Nbr= ", dNum
End Main

Function Real doubleNumber(String message, Integer num1)
      Display message
      Return (num1 * 2)
End Function
```

The below code corrected the error so the first parameter is an Integer and the second is the String:

```
Function Real doubleNumber(Integer num1, String message)
      Display message
      Return (num1 * 2)
End Function
```

**KEY CONCEPT:**

When function returns a value, it does not have to explicitly populate a variable. It can return a value "in-place" and the program will continue to chug along using the returned value.

For example:
```
Display "The new number is: " , calcNumber(number)
```

Another common mistake is to move ALL the code out of a module for no reason. For example, here is part of a short program that did not need to be decomposed any further. The I, P, and O are already separated:

```
Main
      Declare Integer age, newAge
      Display "Please enter your age"
      Input age
      newAge = add50toAge(age)
      displayAgePlus50(newAge)
End Main
```

The student knows they should move as much code out of main as possible, so they do this:

```
Main
      doAllTheWork()
End Main


Module doAllTheWork()
      Declare Integer age, newAge
      Display "Please enter your age"
      Input age
      newAge = add50toAge(age)
      displayAgePlus50(newAge)
End Module
```

See how the code in main is useless now? Is there a programming reason to do that? No. The student does not understand the *purpose* of moving code out of modules and functions.

Look what happens when 3 lines are deleted:

```
Main
      doAllTheWork()
End Main
Module doAllTheWork()
      Declare Integer age, newAge
      Display "Please enter your age"
      Input age
      newAge = add50toAge(age)
      displayAgePlus50(newAge)
End Module Main
```

And we are back to the original program. The takeaway? Create modules whenever you can, but only when it makes sense. You will get better at knowing what makes sense over time and with experience. In the meantime, don't write code like the above example.

Below is another common error. Do you see it?

```
Main
      //other code not shown
      displayName("Bob")
      //other code not shown
End Main

Function String displayName(String value)
      Display value
      Return value
End Function
```

The function returns a value, but the program doesn't DO anything with it. Perhaps the student tried to write a module but incorrectly put a return variable type of "String" in the module header so the compiler insisted this was a function and needed a return statement. So, the student added a return statement, and everything worked! But this is terrible code. The student should have asked themselves if this is a function at all. (It's not!)

When the computer insists you do something, ask yourself if the computer really understands what you are trying to do.

The value a function returns MUST be used. When a function returns a value, either use it or make the function a module.

**KEY CONCEPT:**
Just because a program runs to completion and the output looks correct does not mean it is a good program and will receive a high grade. There are other internal problems for you to solve.
Refer to *Appendix D: Program Checklist*

Writing well-structured programs is part of your assignment and if your program does not follow best practices, your program will not be acceptable.

*"Everything should be made as simple as possible, but not simpler."*
—*Albert Einstein*

## Passing Data to a Module or Function

Data can be passed to modules and functions in two ways.

Pass by **Value** means that only a copy of the argument's value is passed into the module. Changing the variable's value in the module or function will NOT change the original variable's value in the calling routine. This is how data is passed in this textbook.

Pass by **Reference** means that the the address of the variable is passed, not the value, which means the module can modify the value of the original argument. (In this book, and in some software languages such as Java, only arrays are passed by reference.)

In this textbook, we pass variables by value.

Here is an example of passing by value to show how a local variable works:

```
Main

      Declare Integer year = 2020
      Display "In main the year starts as ", year
      displayYear (year)
      Display "Back in main the year is still ", year

End Main

Module displayYear (Integer year)

      year = year + 1111
      Display "In the module the year is ", year

End
```

The output of the above code will be:

```
In main the year starts as 2020
In the module the year is 3131
Back in main the year is still 2020
```

Why didn't *year* change after it was changed in the module? Because the *year* in the module *displayYear(...)* is a local variable and is not the same as the variable named *year* in Main.

To prevent confusion, it is good practice to name the variable in the module's parameter list different from the variable in the calling statement. For example, the above module could have been written this way to avoid confusion:

```
Module displayYear (Integer myYear)
      myYear = myYear + 1111
      Display "In the module the year is ", myYear
End
```

Now it's clear that *year* and *myYear* are two different variables and will have different values.

## Hierarchy Charts

Graphically depicting a program can be especially useful during the design stage of software development. Many software programs are very complicated and so large that the programmer/analyst can't keep everything in their head. Anything that gets information out of your head and into another form will make the task of writing software easier. The more complicated the program, the more analysis work you should do before trying to write one line of code.

A hierarchy chart shows the program's modules and functions by name and which function calls which functions. Coding is much easier when you break up the program into modules before starting to write code. Creating a Hierarchy Chart forces you to think about the program structure before you start to stare at a blank program, not knowing where to begin.

Here is a very basic high-level Hierarchy Chart:

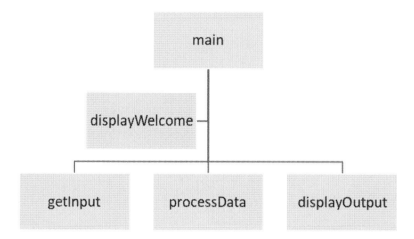

Creating a Hierarchy Chart for a specific problem requires thinking about the problem and deciding what form a solution might take—before writing one line of code. Successful students realize thinking about the problem is important and unsuccessful students think it is a waste of time. Which are you?

 **KEY CONCEPT:**

The more thinking and designing you do before starting to write code, the easier the actual coding will be! If you are frustrated when writing a program, there is no doubt you have not done enough thinking about the problem before trying to code a solution.

Ask yourself, "*What* am I trying to do?" and "*What* has to happen here?"

## IPO Charts

Once you have created a Hierarchy Chart when analyzing a problem and designing a solution, another useful tool, especially when you are creating program specifications for another programmer, is the *IPO chart*. An IPO chart shows the Input/Processing/Output that is done in each module and function. From this, you should be able to easily write the code for the program.

Below is an example of a function that... does what?

| calculateSumOf3Integers | | |
|---|---|---|
| Input | Processing | Output |
| Three integers | Add the three integers together | Return the sum of the three integers |

It calculates the sum of three integers! How do you think I knew that? It's not magic when you name your functions correctly. This function takes in three Integers as parameters, adds them together, and returns the sum of the three.

Can you write this function? Give it a try before looking below!

```
Function Integer calculateSumOf3Integers (Integer nbr1,
                                           Integer nbr2,
                                           Integer nbr3)

        Declare Integer total
        total = nbr1 + nbr2 + nbr3
        Return total
End Function
```

A shorter way to write the function is this way...

```
Function Integer calculateSumOf3Integers (Integer nbr1,
                                           Integer nbr2,
                                           Integer nbr3)

        Return (nbr1 + nbr2 + nbr3)
End Function
```

## Analysis and Programming

If you are hired as a programmer, you will be given small programming tasks to prove you know what you claim to know. Someone else may do the analysis and give you Hierarchy Charts, IPO Charts, program specifications, test plans, and other program documentation for you to study before you code the program.

But, as you gain experience, you will not always be doing programming work. Sometimes you will analyze a problem and document the solution for another programmer. You won't write the code at all. You'll start to create Hierarchy Charts, IPO Charts, program specifications, test plans, and other program documentation for other programmers to use in writing code. Your job will be to think, not to write code.

This is why at the beginning of your education in computer science it is a mistake to try to write code without at least attempting to create a Hierarchy Chart, a test plan, and an IPO chart for the critical modules and functions. You will need to be able to use these tools in your future job and the more practice you have with them now, the more effective you will be as an employee.

## Library Functions

Every software language has built-in library functions that have already been written for you. Using library functions will save A LOT of time. You don't have to write a function that returns a random number; you don't have to write a function that turns text into uppercase; you don't have to write a function that returns a substring of a String—those have already been written for you!

Library functions are functions: you send them data, and they return a value back to you. And you didn't have to write the code inside the function!

It is your responsibility to become familiar with the available library functions for your language. To begin I suggest studying String functions because manipulating strings is a common task you will have to do repeatedly in classes and during your professional career.

If you do not become very familiar with the available library functions for the software language you are working in, you may not be able to solve the problem you are trying to solve or you will use a lot more time than you needed to use.

Coding Exercise:

In a specific software language such as Java, Python, C, C++, or C#, do the following and display the result to the user.

1. Define this string: "This is a String".
2. Display the length of the string.
3. Convert the string to uppercase and display it.
4. Convert the string to lowercase and display it.
5. Using a substring function, display the first 7 characters of the string.
6. Get a random number and display it.

## Developing a getRandomNumber Function

All programming languages have a way to generate a random number. Well, that's not quite true. No software can generate a truly random number—the closest software can do is to generate a good-enough random number.

Here is a pseudocode method to get a random number: (programming languages will differ slightly)

```
randomNumber = Math.random()
```

The Math function will return a value from 0 to 1, not including 1. But what if you want an integer from 0 to 100? The calling program will have to convert the return value using a mathematical formula such as this:

```
Declare Integer randomNumber
randomNumber = Math.random() * 100
```

And every time a program needs a random number that does not start with 0, such as a random number from 10 to 20, you will have to write a conversion in the program over and over again. That's a waste of your valuable time. To generalize the function, let's do those conversions in a getRandomNumber() function instead.

**A Thinking and Coding Exercise:**

Create a function named **getRandomNumber (low, high)** that will pass the lowest and the highest value the program wants generated, and then use those values to generate and return a random number between those numbers, inclusive.

This is an analysis task and, to show your solution works, you will put this in code. This is a good example of the type of analysis and problem solving software developers have to be able to do on their own.

Here is a suggestion on how to solve this: first try just using the low value to restrict the random number, then work on restricting the formula to the high value.

Give it a try!

| getRandomNumber | | |
|---|---|---|
| Input | Processing | Output |
| Two integers: low and high | Generate a random number between the low and high numbers, inclusive of each | Return a random number between the input parameters, inclusive |

This is not an easy exercise. Take your time.

Assume Math.Random() returns a Real number from 0 to 1, not including the number 1. And it will come in handy to remember the concept of integer truncation for this problem! (page 43)

Here is one solution:

```
Function Integer getRandomNumber(Integer low, Integer high)

    Declare Integer randomNbr
    randomNbr = (Math.random() * ((high + 1) - low)) + low;
    Return randomNbr

End Function
```

Let's test that code by plugging in some sample numbers.

When we want a random number from 11 to 22, including 11 and 22, here is how the math works out:

```
(Math.random() * ((22 + 1) - 11)) + 11

(Math.random() * (23 - 11)) + 11

(Math.random() *  12) + 11
```

Now let's imagine the Math.random function returns extreme values: 0 and then .999

First let's plug in 0:

```
(0 * 12) + 11
(0) + 11
11
```

So, the number 11 is the lowest value that will be returned.

Now let's plug in .999:

```
(.999 * 12) + 11
(11.998) + 11
22.998
22
```

And returning an Integer will strip off the numbers to the right of the decimal, so 22 is the highest value that will be returned.

Success!

--------------------

If you are wondering what the teacher wants from your program...

- Refer to the list of **qualities of good code** on page 21.
- Refer to the list of **expectations for the user-interface** on page 26.
- Refer to the list of **internal program expectations** on page 26.
- Refer to *Appendix C: Testplan Checklist* and to *Appendix D: Program Checklist* for a structured method of reviewing your program's code.

## Generalized Modules and Functions

When 100 modules are exactly alike, there is no reason to have 100 modules. Create one *generalized module* and use that instead. A generalized module will save you time in coding, debugging, and maintaining your code.

Here is an example of code that works, but is badly written—something a beginner might write:

```
//This program uses 3 functions to get 3 types of names.
Main
      Declare String fName, mName, lName
      fName = getFirstName()
      mName = getMiddleName()
      lName = getLastName()
      displayName(fName, mName, lName)
End Main
```

Here are three Modules that are not generalized. Notice they all do the same thing.
Change the variable names and the question text and they are EXACTLY the same.

```
Function String getFirstName ()
      Declare String firstName
      Display "Please enter your first name."
      Input  firstName
      Return firstName
End Function

Function String getMiddleName ()
      Declare String middleName
      Display "Please enter your middle name."
      Input  middleName
      Return middleName
End Function

Function String getLastName ()
      Declare String lastName
      Display "Please enter your last name."
      Input  lastName
      Return lastName
End Function

Module displayName(String first, String middle, String last)
      Display "Your name is: " first, " ", middle, " ", Last
End Module
```

Here is the Hierarchy Chart for the above program:

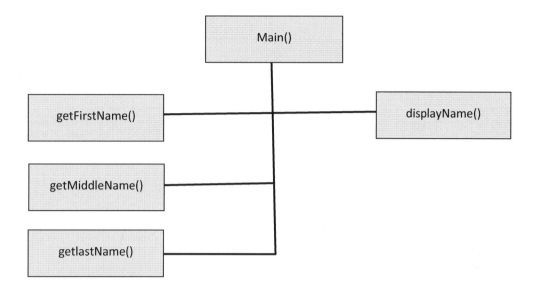

Let's rewrite the code above to use a generalized input function that returns a string.

```
Main
      Declare String fName, mName, lName

      fName = getString("Please enter your first name")
      mName = getString("Please enter your middle name")
      lName = getString("Please enter your last name")

      displayName(fName, mName, lName)
End Main
```

This generalized function displays the message received from a parameter:

```
Function String getString (String msg)
      Declare String newValue

      Display msg
      Input  newValue

      Return newValue
End Function
```

Notice how three functions were replaced by one generalized function. And this one *getString* function can be used to return ANY string in ANY program! We have passed into the function the message so the function can be used to ask for any String value. This is called *reusable code* and it will save you time later.

Here is the Hierarchy Chart for the above program:

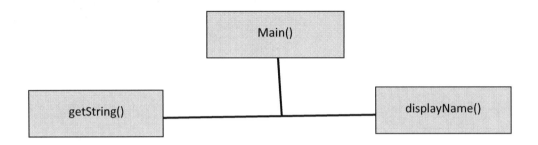

Much simpler, and easier to maintain over time.

It is good form to strive to write reusable code every time you create a program. Great programmers have a large personal library of code they have written that they can use to create new programs quickly and efficiently.

> *"It should be noted that no ethically-trained software engineer would ever consent to write a **destroyBaghdad** procedure. Basic professional ethics would instead require him to write a **destroyCity** procedure, to which Baghdad could be given as a parameter."*
>
> —*Nathaniel Borenstein*

## Evolution of Generalized Input Functions: Part 1

As you learn more programming structures and techniques in this book, we will enhance the input functions you use in your programs. Before this chapter, all the code you wrote was in the main part of the program. Now that you know how to write functions, and you understand how useful generalized functions are, we will create generalized input functions for you to use.

Until the next chapter is covered, review and use these generalized input functions:

```
Function String getString (String msg)
      Declare String newValue
      Display msg
      Input newValue
      Return newValue
End Function

Function Integer getInteger (String msg)
      Declare Integer newValue
      Display msg
      Input newValue
      Return newValue
End Function

Function Real getReal (String msg)
      Declare Real newValue
      Display msg
      Input newValue
      Return newValue
End Function
```

Notice that the *getInteger (...)* function above returns an Integer, which makes sense, right? And the *getReal (...)* function returns a Real number. The function header, as always, tells the computer what kind of variable is being returned. Here is how to call one of the above functions.

```
Declare String userName
userName = getString ("Please enter your name")
Display "The string you entered was: ", userName
```

As an exercise, identify the parts of the three functions above that are different from each other. You don't have to memorize all these functions. Once you understand one, the others are the same with different variable types.

## Program Structures: IPO with Modules and Functions

There are good program structures and bad program structures. Fortunately, you don't have to reinvent program structures that computer scientists have already created. You just have to use them.

Notice below how the data flows from the *getString(...)* function to the variable *username*, to the argument for *getInteger(...)*, to the variable *age*, to a formula, and finally to the argument for the module *displayAge(...)*. This program follows the IPO structure using two functions and a module.

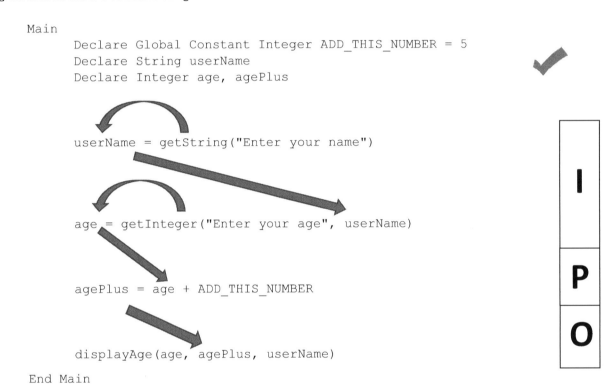

Note that the processing line is not a function because it is only 1 line. One-line functions are not very useful so I kept the one processing line in main.

**KEY CONCEPT:**
Most of the programs and functions you write will follow the IPO structure shown above. Learn it!

Did you follow and understand all the above information? If not, study and ask questions until you understand it. Try teaching it to a fellow student. You have to understand this before you go on to the next chapter!

## Review Questions

You should be able to answer these questions, discuss their meaning, and give an example. Pretend you are in a job interview—you should know the answers, right?

1.  What is the difference between a module and a function?

2.  What are the parts of a function header?

3.  What is a global constant?

4.  What is an argument?

5.  What are parameters?

6.  What happens if the argument list and the parameter don't match exactly?

7.  What does a return statement do?

8.  How should modules and functions be named?

9.  How many things should a module or function do?

10. What is scope?

11. What does *passing by value* mean?  What does *passing by reference* mean?

12. What is a Hierarchy Chart?

13. What is an IPO Chart?

14. What are library functions?

15. What is a generalized function?

## Can You Do This?

1.  Write the below three generalized input functions from memory and from your understanding of how functions work.

    ```
    getInteger (…)
    getString (…)
    getReal (…)
    ```

    If you cannot do this, first copy the routines while looking at them.
    Then try to write them from memory.

    If you still have trouble doing this, try copying 1 line and writing that from memory. Repeat for all the lines.

2.  How can a program use the *getRandomNumber (…)* function in this chapter to generate a number between 5.00 and 6.00 (for example: 5.01, 5.52, 5.60, 5.76, 5.99, etc) since the function returns only Integers?

    Code your solution in a programming language such as Java, Python, C, C++, or C# and display 20 random numbers between 5 and 6.

    --------------------------

Can you do the above? Computer Science is not a subject where you can catch up later. You must stay up to date with your reading and understanding so you are always ready to learn the next concept.

> Now is a good time to go back and review *Chapter 3: Solving Problems*. The testing and debugging strategies discussed in that chapter will make more sense to you now.

# Chapter 6
# Decision Structures and Boolean Logic

Most programs must make decisions like these:

```
If this is equal to that
     do this.

If this is not equal to that and this thing is equal to that thing,
     do this.

If this is greater than that,
     do this,
Else
     do that.
```

## Terminology You must Know

As you read this chapter, be sure you learn the definition and reason why the below terms are important. Define and describe each of the below terms out loud. If you can't define a word out loud, you don't really know it!

| | | | |
|---|---|---|---|
| If | == | < | NOT |
| Else | != | <= | Boolean values |
| Select | > | AND | Modulus |
| Case | >= | OR | Default |
| Break | | | |

## Sample Pseudocode

By the end of the chapter you must be able to read and write each of these lines of code like the below examples before you move onto the next chapter. (This is not a program).

```
If employeeType == HOURLY
If employeeType == SALARIED AND employeeSalary > 100000

Select (variableToEvaluate)
     Case 1: x = 14;
     Default:
          Break
End Select
```

## Relational Operators

Decision structures use relational operators to make comparisons that result in a Boolean value of True or False.

| Operator | Means |
|---|---|
| == | Equal to |
| > | Greater than |
| < | Less than |
| >= | Greater than or Equal to |
| <= | Less than or Equal to |
| != | Not Equal to |

The result of a comparison is either true or false. Here are some coding examples and what they mean:

| | |
|---|---|
| If a == b | Is a is equal to b? If so, the result is true. |
| If a > b | Is a is greater than b? |
| If a < b | Is a is less than b? |
| If a >= b | Is a is greater than or equal to b? |
| If a <= b | Is a is less than or equal to b? |
| If a != b | Is a is not equal to b? |

Note the difference between == and =. The single = is an assignment operator in formulas. The double == is a comparison operator. If-statements use the == operator.

Here is the basic structure of a simple if-statement:

```
If (this condition is true)
      //execute these lines of code
End If
```

Below are examples of simple if-statements in a program. Notice the way the "insides" of the If-statement is indented. Standard indenting gives the programmer a quick visual understanding of the code.

```
Main
      Declare Integer age
      Display "Please enter your age"
      Input age

      If age < 19   //if this is true, execute the below line
            Display "You're a minor"
      End If

      If age > 18
            Display "You're an adult"
      End If
End Main
```

Note that each if-statement ends in an *End If* statement.

Here is another way to write the above code that uses an *Else* statement. If the first statement is true in the if-statement, the computer executes it, otherwise, it goes to the *else* statement and keeps running.

```
Main
      Declare Integer age
      Display "Please enter your age"
      Input age

      If age < 18
            Display "You're a minor"      //the condition is true
      Else
            Display "You're an adult"     //the condition is false
      End If
End Main
```

If-statements can be nested inside each other. Notice each if-statement has a matching End-If statement. Also, notice the indentions inside each if-statement. Proper indentions of three or more characters are important for readability. Indenting one or two characters is not enough!

```
Main
      Declare Integer age
      Display "Please enter your age"
      Input age

      If age < 18
            Display "You're a minor"
      Else
            If age >= 65
                  Display "You're a senior citizen"
            Else
                  Display "You're an adult"
            End If
      End If
End Main
```

Below is another way to nest the if-statements. This is called an *if-else-if* structure and it requires fewer end-if statements.

```
Main
      Declare Integer age
      Display "Please enter your age"
      Input age

      If age < 18
            Display "You're a minor"
      Else  If age >= 65
            Display "You're a senior citizen"
      Else
            Display "You're an adult"
      End If
End Main
```

## Logical Operators

Programmers use logical operators ALL THE TIME. (Detect a pattern here? You can't ignore ANYTHING in a programming book. You will use it all sooner or later!

**KEY CONCEPTS:**

Logical operators you must know:

- AND – Both conditions must be true
- OR – Either condition must be true
- NOT – Reverses the truth of an expression

If-statements can be combined using logical operators like this:

```
If userAge < 18 OR userAge > 65

If userName == "unknown" AND userAge == 0

If salary > 10000 AND employeeType == "M"
```

Below are the basic truth tables using Boolean values of True and False. The first line says: if A is true and B is true, then A AND B is true.

| A | B | A AND B |
|---|---|---------|
| T | T | T |
| T | F | F |
| F | T | F |
| F | F | F |

| A | B | A OR B |
|---|---|--------|
| T | T | T |
| T | F | T |
| F | T | T |
| F | F | F |

If you have trouble conceptualizing a complicated logical expression, imagine a concrete example. For example, to determine if *False OR True* results in a True or False answer, say a two-part statement with the first part is False, and the second part is True, like this:

I am a dog OR I am a human

I am not a dog (False), but I am a human (True).  So, the entire statement is True because one of the statements is True.

Let's try another:

I am a dog OR I am a cat

The answer is False to both and the answer to the compound condition is also False: I am not a dog OR a cat.

-----------------------------

The **NOT** operator just reverses the value of what it is operating on. Let's try one:

NOT (True)

This statement resolves to False.

Here is another:

False OR (Not False) OR False

This statement resolves to True!

-----------------------------

Now check this out:

```
If (a >= b)
```

is logically equivalent to

```
If (a > b OR a == b)
```

Knowing this kind of translation will come in handy when writing programs that are comparing values. (Which is almost all of them).

## Common Boolean Errors

Here are some common errors that will prevent you from being hired anywhere:

What's wrong with this code?

```
If myBoolean = true
```

The = sign, the assignment operator, puts the true value into the myBoolean variable so the if-statement is ALWAYS true!

What's wrong with this code? After all, the student changed the = sign to the relational operator ==.

```
If myBoolean == true
```

The above code will run correctly but doing this identifies you as an amateur. You don't have to compare a Boolean value to true or false—they ARE true or false already. The correct way to write Boolean if-statements is like this:

```
If myBoolean
```

Ta-da! Nothing else is needed!  The variable myBoolean IS true or false already. It doesn't need to be explicitly compared to true or false.

## Common Errors

Suppose you want to check if a number is greater than 30 but less than 40? Here is the correctly coded if-statement:

```
If num > 30 AND num < 40
```

Here are some common errors made trying to write the above if-statement:

```
If num > 30 OR num < 40     //All numbers are > 30 OR < 40

If num >= 30 AND num <= 40  //This includes 30 and 40

If num > 30 AND < 40        //This is a syntax error
```

A common error, even for professionals, is to type > when they meant to type >= or they typed <= and they program requires <. The professional knows that Relational operators are a common source of errors so they will give their code another look after typing it in to make sure the if-statement is doing what it is supposed to do and fix it if it is wrong. Beginners, on the other hand, will type their code and assume whatever golden code they typed is correct and never go back to review it.

> **KEY CONCEPT:**
>
> All programmers make errors. The cool thing about programming is that we can fix our errors. The super-programmer will fix their errors very quickly. The beginner will not even look at the code to determine if there is an error or not.
>
> When a beginning student looks at their code and sees an error, they may take a long time to fix it. This is OK. They will get faster. The important thing is to find the errors and not assume your code, because you wrote it, is always correct.

Here is a common Pseudocode error that some beginning programmers make:

```
If num > 30 AND num < 40

        //do something

Display "The next Line"
```

The if-statement is missing the *End-If* statement. In many languages, such as the pseudocode in this book, a block of code has a starting point and an ending point. In Java and Javascript, *brackets* start and end blocks of code: { //code goes here }

In Pseudocode If-statements must end with an *End-If* statement like this:

```
If num > 30 AND num < 40
        //do something
End If
Display "The next Line"
```

---

**FLASHBACK!**

Remember that your programs MUST be indented properly so you can more easily write the code, read the code, and debug the code.

If-statements have a proper indented structure to follow.

---

Sometimes an error does not cause the program to crash or to run incorrectly, it's just really annoying for anyone reading the code. Look at how this code is formatted and indented:

```
Module displayData (  Integer            theValue        )
      If        theValue        ==        0
   Display                "Equals zero"
               Else
      If theValue              >                              0
          Display "Greater than zero"
                          Else
Display "Less than zero"
End                             If
          End                   If
End Module
```

Why would anyone indent their code this way? Is that code easy to read? No.

Some languages, such as Python, require the indentions to be correct or the program will not run correctly!

Here is the code properly indented. Isn't this code easier to read?

```
Module displayData (Integer theValue)
      If theValue == 0
            Display "Equals zero"
      Else
            If theValue > 0
                  Display "Greater than zero"
            Else
                  Display "Less than zero"
            End If
      End If
End Module
```

Note how much easier it is to tell what happens during each condition. You barely have to read the code because you can rely upon the indentions to tell you information about the intent of the code.

Professionals can tell a program is well-structured and properly indented from across the room. And they can tell if a program is not well-structured in the same way. Guess which programmer gets the job or gets to keep their job?

In most Integrated Development Environments (IDE) you can automatically indent your code. Inside your IDE, select all lines of code (perhaps using CTRL-A) and then press tab, or something similar, to automatically indent your code. Don't ignore this functionality—use it!

## Comparing Strings

Do you have any pictures inside your smartphone? Or any music? The answer is no, you don't. If you break open your phone, you will not find any pictures or music. Everything inside a computer is stored as zeros or ones. Software translates a bunch of ones and zeros to show a picture or produce music for the speaker to play. It is like magic to people who don't know how a computer really works.

Can a program compare pictures? Is it possible to ask:

```
If pictureOne > pictureTwo
```

Yes, it is. Everything in a computer is ones and zeros.

Strings can be compared to each other since they resolve to the numbers 0 and 1 anyway. How else could a computer sort a list of song titles or a list of employees by last name? Here is how it looks in pseudocode:

```
If favoriteMusicalGroup == "Weird Al"
        //question your musical taste here
End If
```

Note: In some languages, like Java, you can't use == to compare Strings.
In Java you have to use the String *equals*() function:

```
if (myString.equals("B")) {
```

"Why is that?" you might ask. The reason for this is because strings are Objects and the string variable name points to the object that contains the value of the string. When you compare strings with == you are comparing their memory locations and not the contents of the string itself.

Aren't you glad you asked? Don't worry, you don't have to know that for this introductory class, but you will need to understand it later when you take a class that does not use pseudocode.

### Converting Strings

Strings can be converted to numbers and numbers can be converted to Strings.

```
Declare Real myNumber = 3.1415
Declare String aNumber = "" + myNumber
```

And Strings can be converted to numbers also using library functions, like this:

```
Declare String myString = "3.1415"
Declare Real aNumber = stringToReal(myNumber)
```

## The If-Else-If statement

You have seen if-statements, and if-else statements, and now here is another example of if-else-if statement.

```
If dogName == "Spot"
      Display "Come Spot!"
Else
      If dogName == "Fido"
            Display "Come Fido"
      Else
            If dogName == "Lassie"
                  Display "Come Lassie"
            Else
                  If dogName == "Rin-Tin-Tin"
                        Display "Come Tin-Tin"
                  Else
                        If dogGender == MALE
                              Display "Come boy!"
                        Else
                              Display "Come girl!"
                        End If
                  End If
            End If
      End If
End If
```

Imagine we had 10 more dog names to call. The if-statements would go off the page entirely. But don't worry! The code above can be structured like below, using the if-else-if structure:

```
If dogName == "Spot"
      Display "Come Spot!"
Else If dogName == "Fido"
      Display "Come Fido"
Else If dogName == "Lassie"
      Display "Come Lassie"
Else If dogName == "Rin-Tin-Tin"
      Display "Come Rin-Tin-Tin"
Else If dogGender == MALE
      Display "Come boy!"
Else
      Display "Come girl!"
End If
```

Which is the best form to use? It depends on how many if-statements you have and if they run off the screen to the right. Use whichever form is easiest for you to maintain and debug. The computer will not care.

**A Mental Exercise:**

What's wrong with this If-statement? How would you rewrite it?

```
If score > 90 AND score < 100
    grade = "A"
Else If score > 80 AND score <= 89
    grade = "B"
Else If score > 70 AND score <= 79
    grade = "C"
Else If score > 60 AND score <= 69
    grade = "D"
Else If score > 0 AND score <= 59
    grade = "F"
End If
```

Hint: Imagine various values for *score* and see what happens. What values should you test with? Think about it! The answer to this will be at the end of the chapter.

You never fail until you stop trying."
—*Albert Einstein*

You can do this if you don't give up!

## The Select-Case Structure: Creating a Menu

There is another decision structure that is used ALL THE TIME in programming: The Select-Case structure. Your specific programming language may use slightly different names and that's OK. Every language wants to be different from other languages, but they all use the same basic concepts you're learning in this book.

A select statement evaluates a variable and executes a "case" when it equals the value of the variable. The "case" ends with a break statement. This book will use explicit "Break" statements to end the case in the select structure. If there is no *Break* in the case, then the next line is executed. Note that in Case 4 below, there is no break statement. That means Case 4 will execute *goDoTheFourthThing*() and *goDoTheFifthThing*() before exiting the structure.

Here is how to use a select-case structure as a simple one-time menu: (with poorly worded modules!)

```
Declare Integer menuOption
menuOption = getInteger("Please enter your choice")
Select (menuOption)
      Case 1:
            goDoSomething()
            Break
      Case 2:
            goDoSomethingElse()
            Break
      Case 3:
            goDoTheThirdThing()
            Break
      Case 4:
            goDoTheFourthThing()
      Case 5:
            goDoTheFifthThing()
            Break
      Default:
            Display "Invalid menu option"
            Break
End Select
```

The Default case is used if none of the case statements were selected because menuOption did not equal 1, 2, 3, 4, or 5.

See how the Select-Case structure tidies up the code? Now imagine you have 20 different cases—that would really show how beneficial the Select-Case model is over a long string of if-statements.

The case statement is useful for testing equality, but it cannot be used with > or < comparisons. For those comparisons, use an if-statement.

Select-Case Exercise:

> For these values of *myNumber*, determine the value of the variable *myNumber* after this code is executed. The answers will be at the end of the chapter.

1. myNumber = 0
2. myNumber = 5
3. myNumber = 10
4. myNumber = 15
5. myNumber = 25
6. myNumber = 30

```
Select (myNumber)
     Case 0:
            myNumber = myNumber + 1
            Break
     Case 5:
     Case 6:
            myNumber++
     Case 10:
            If myNumber == 6
                  myNumber = 25
            Else
                  myNumber++
            End If
            Break
     Case 15:
            myNumber = myNumber
     Case 20:
            Break
     Case 25:
            myNumber = myNumber - 1
     Case 50:
            myNumber = myNumber + 10
            Break
     Default:
            myNumber = 0
            Break
End Select

Display "The result is: ", myNumber
```

## Modulus

Modulus, the calculation of the remainder after a division, is probably not used in your every-day life, but the modulus function is important for programmers to know.

An example: 12 MOD 4 is 0 since 12 divided by 4 is 3 with nothing left over.

Let's try another. 17 MOD 5 is 2 since 17 divided by 5 is 3 with 2 left over.

Some uses of modulus include clock arithmetic, determining leap years, boundary checking, determining if a number is even or odd, and getting a specific digit of a number.

**KEY CONCEPT:**

The modulus function divides one number by another and returns the remainder.

Modulus is a very handy mathematical tool for programmers. Become comfortable with using it and you will find even more uses for it.

Here are more examples of using Modulus:

| | |
|---|---|
| 10 MOD 1 = 0 | 10 divided by 1 is 10 with 0 left over. |
| 10 MOD 2 = 0 | |
| 10 MOD 3 = 1 | 10 divided by 3 is 3 with 1 left over. |
| 10 MOD 4 = 2 | 10 divided by 4 is 2 with 2 left over. |
| 10 MOD 5 = 0 | |
| 10 MOD 6 = 4 | |
| 10 MOD 7 = 3 | 10 divided by 7 is 1 with 3 left over. |
| 10 MOD 8 = 2 | |
| 10 MOD 9 = 1 | |
| 9 MOD 5 = 4 | |
| 299 MOD 150 = 149 | Can you follow the pattern? |

Here is an example of how to use modulus in an if-statement:

```
If (myNumber MOD 10 == 0)
      Display "This number is evenly divisible by 10"
Else
      Display "This number is NOT evenly divisible by 10"
End If
```

## Evolution of Generalized Input Functions: Part 2 – Checking for Invalid Data

As you learn more programming structures and techniques in this book, we will enhance the generalized input functions you will use in your programs. Now that you know how to write if-statements, we can modify our generalized input functions to check for invalid data entered by the user.

Until the next chapter is covered, review, study, and use these generalized input functions:

```
Function String getString (String msg)
        Declare String newValue
        Display msg
        Input newValue
        If newValue is null or spaces
                Display "Invalid entry"
                Stop Program
        End If
        Return newValue
End Function
```

```
Function Integer getInteger (String msg)
        Declare Integer newValue
        Display msg
        Input newValue
        If newValue is not an Integer
                Display "Invalid number"
                Stop Program
        End If
        Return newValue
End Function
```

```
Function Real getReal (String msg)
        Declare Real newValue
        Display msg
        Input newValue
        If newValue is not a Real number
                Display "Invalid number"
                Stop Program
        End If
        Return newValue
End Function
```

As a mental exercise, identify the parts of the three functions above that are different from each other. You don't have to memorize all these functions. Once you understand one, the others are the same.

The generalized input validation functions are used the same way as any function:

```
Main
     Declare Integer myInteger
     myInteger = getInteger ("Please enter your age")
     Display "The number you entered was: ", myInteger
End Main
```

Coding Exercise:

Convert the above 3 pseudocode functions and the associated calling statements in a specific programming language such as Java, Python, C, C++, or C#.

Now, look at the below function. It asks the user to enter Y or N using the generalized *getString(...)* function.

```
Function Boolean getYesOrNo (String msg)
       Declare String newValue
       newValue = getString(msg)
       If uppercase(newValue) is not "Y"
         AND uppercase(newValue) is not "N"
             Display "Invalid entry. Should be Y or N"
             Stop Program
             //we stop since we haven't learned loops yet
       End If
       If newValue is "Y"
             Return true
       End If
       Return false
End Function
```

Notice that *getYesOrNo(...)* uses *getString(...)*. Why is that? Because *getString(...)* is a generalized input function that can return any kind of string such as Y or N. See how useful that is?

-------------------

If you are wondering what the teacher wants from your program...

- Refer to the list of **qualities of good code** on page 21.
- Refer to the list of **expectations for the user-interface** on page 26.
- Refer to the list of **internal program expectations** on page 26.

Refer to *Appendix C: Testplan Checklist* and to *Appendix D: Program Checklist* for a structured method of reviewing your program's code.

## Removing Code from Main

It's possible to write small programs with all the code is in main, but that's not good practice for the larger and more complicated programs you will eventually write. You should strive to remove as much code from main as possible, within reason, and when there is a reason to do so.

Ask yourself, can I move any code from main to its own function? Good candidates for moving are entire if-statements, or the code inside each branch of an if-statement. Here are some examples:  (these are code snippets, not entire programs)

```
Main
      //other code not shown
      Declare Boolean playerWins
      playerWins = playGame()
      If playerWins
            DisplayVictoryMessage()
      Else
            DisplayDefeatMessage()
      End If
      //other code not shown
End Main
```

The if-statement above could be replaced entirely like this:

```
Main
      //other code not shown

      Declare Boolean playerWins
      playerWins = playGame()
      displayGameResult(playerWins)

      //other code not shown
End Main
```

The if-statement is now in the *displayGameResult*(...) module.

Look at the above program and see that you can read the code in main and know what the program does:
1.    The player plays the game
2.    And then the result of the game is displayed.

Being able to read the function names and understand what the program does is one of the goals of moving code out of main or any function.

The below code snippet shows how to move code from a more complicated if-statement while keeping the control structure.

```
Main
      //other code not shown
      employeeID = getEmployeeID()
      If employeeIsActive(employeeID)
            updateEmployeeBenefits(employeeID)
            updateEmpoyeeVacationSchedule(employeeID)
            If getEmployeeType(employeeID) == EXEMPT
                  updateSpecialReport(employeeID)
            End If
            writeEmployeeToReport(employeeID)
      Else
            writeEmployeeToExceptionReport(employeeID)
      End If
      //other code not shown
End Main
```

Here is main with <u>most</u> of the code moved to another module:

```
Main
      //other code not shown
      employeeID = getEmployeeID()
      If employeeIsActive(employeeID)
            UpdateEmployeeData(employeeID)
            writeEmployeeToReport(employeeID)
      Else
            writeEmployeeToExceptionReport(employeeID)
      End If
      //other code not shown
End Main
```

Here it is with <u>all</u> the code moved to another module:

```
Main
      //other code not shown
      employeeID = getEmployeeID()
      UpdateEmployeeData(employeeID)
      //other code not shown
End Main
```

How much code should you take out of main, or out of any other function? As much as you can when it makes sense. You will get a feel for this as you write more programs, but, until then, when in doubt, move the code to another function.

## Answers to Exercises in this Chapter

**Answer to If-Statement Exercise:**

The if-statement does not handle the boundary conditions correctly. Test with 100 and 90 and you will see that it needed to be rewritten. Here are three solutions: (all of them are correct)

```
If score >= 90
    grade = "A"
Else If score >= 80
    grade = "B"
Else If score >= 70
    grade = "C"
Else If score >= 60
    grade = "D"
Else
    grade = "F"
End If

//-----------------------------------------------------------

If score < 60
    grade = "F"
Else If score < 70
    grade = "D"
Else If score < 80
    grade = "C"
Else If score < 90
    grade = "B"
Else
    grade = "A"
End If

//-----------------------------------------------------------

If score < 60
    grade = "F"
Else
        If score < 70
            grade = "D"
        Else
            If score < 80
                grade = "C"
            Else
                If score < 90
                    grade = "B"
                Else
                    grade = "A"
                End If
            End If
        End If
End If
```

**Answer to Select-Case exercise:**

After the code runs, the value of myNumber will be:

1.  myNumber = 1
2.  myNumber = 25
3.  myNumber = 11
4.  myNumber = 15
5.  myNumber = 34
6.  myNumber = 0

If you did not get the correct answer for EVERY value, do it again until you do.

You don't want to struggle with this when you have a real problem to solve!

*"Any fool can know. The point is to understand."*

*—Albert Einstein*

*When you look up an answer, you can only know the answer.*
*To understand you must think and develop the answer yourself.*

Refer to *Design and then Code* on page 50.

Now is a good time to go back and review *Chapter 3: Solving Problems*. The testing and debugging strategies discussed in that chapter will make more sense to you

## Review Questions

You should be able to answer these questions, discuss their meaning, and give examples. Pretend you are in a job interview—you should know the answers, right?

1. What are relational operators? Give examples.

2. Do if-statements have to end in some way? If so, how?

3. Describe how the code in if-statements is indented.

4. What is a logical operator? Give three examples.

5. Is this a proper if-statement?    `If (myBoolean == true)`

6. What is wrong with this code?    `If num > 10 OR num < 100`

7. What is a select-case structure? Describe all the parts.

8. What is modulus?

9. What are the results of these formulas?

   a. `50 MOD 20`

   b. `1000 MOD 300`

   c. `17 MOD 3`

   d. `33 MOD 2`

   e. `2000 MOD 2`

10. What do these Boolean expressions resolve to: True or False?

    a. `True OR False`

    b. `False OR False`

    c. `True AND False`

    d. `False AND False`

    e. `NOT True OR False`

    f. `NOT True AND NOT False`

    g. `NOT False OR NOT True`

    h. `True AND (False OR True) OR False`

## Can You Do This?

1.  Close this book and write in pseudocode the below four generalized input functions from memory and from your understanding of how functions work.

    ```
    getString(…)
    getInteger(…)
    getReal(…)
    getYesOrNo(…)
    ```

    If you cannot do this, first copy the routines while looking at them.
    Then try to write them from memory.

    If you still have trouble doing this, try copying 1 line at a time and writing that from memory. Do what you have to do to learn these functions!

2.  Do the following:
    a. Write one if-statement that checks if an integer is greater than zero, not equal to 10 or 50, and less than 99.
       If the number meets all those requirements, display "It's OK!", otherwise display "Bad number!".
    b. Write the above using multiple nested if-statements.

3.  Do the following:
    a. Write a function in pseudocode that determines if a number is even or odd.
       The IPO Chart for this is below.

    b. Write a program in a programming language such as Java, Python, C, C++, or C# to demonstrate how it works.

| isEven | | |
|---|---|---|
| **Input** | **Processing** | **Output** |
| One integer | Use MOD.<br>Think about how to do this! | Returns true if the number is even.<br><br>Returns false if the number is odd. |

The calling statement will look like this:

```
If (isEven(numberToCheck))
```

I'm on step 12, the last step, but it says to go back to the first step!

# Chapter 7
# Loops

You have already used loops as a user of technology. Anytime you have repeated an action, you were using a loop. When you type your password incorrectly and the software program asks you to try again—that's a loop. Loops are very useful and are used all the time in programming.

This book covers three types of loops:

The Do-While Loop:

```
//this loop continues while the condition is true
Do                 //starts a do-while loop (a post-test loop)
                   //code inside the loop goes here
While (x <= 10)    //ends the do-while loop.
```

The While-loop:

```
//this loop continues while the condition is true
While (x <= 10)    //starts the do-while loop (a pre-test loop)
                   //code inside the loop goes here
End While          //ends the while-loop
```

The For-loop:

```
For x = 1 to 10    //starts the for-loop (a pre-test loop)
                   //code inside the loop goes here
End For            //ends the for-loop
```

This is where you really start to learn about following models of code instead of re-inventing the wheel every time you need to write a loop. I am going to show you the basic loops you will use in your programs. These are the tools you need to know how to use without thinking about how to write them. Study the models and learn how they work so you can code all of them without having to re-invent their structure. This is not plagiarizing—when we use code others have created, we stand on the shoulders of giants!

## Terminology You must Know

As you read this chapter, be sure you learn the definition and reason why the below terms are important. Define and describe each of the below terms out loud. If you can't define a word out loud, you don't really know it! You need to know these terms so you can talk about your code with others.

| | | | |
|---|---|---|---|
| Do-while-loop | pre-test loop | initialization | total |
| While-loop | post-test loop | counter | wantsToContinue loop |
| For-loop | sentinel | increment | game loop |
| nested loops | infinite loop | decrement | counting loop |

## Sample Pseudocode

By the end of the chapter, you must be able to read and write each of these lines of code before you move onto the next chapter.

```
Do                      //starts a do-while loop
While (x < 10)          //starts while-loop or ends a do-while loop
For x = 1 to MAX Step 1 //starts a for-loop, increments by 1
```

## A Counting Loop

Do you need to do something a number of times? Below is a pre-test loop:

```
//Pre-test Loop with a counter
Declare Integer last, counter
last = 99
counter = 0

While (counter <= last) //keeps looping while this is true
     //code inside loop goes here. May never be executed.
     counter = counter + 1   //or use counter++

End While

Display "The loop ran ", counter, " times."
```

Here is another way to count using a post-test loop:

```
//Post-test Loop with a counter
Declare Integer last, counter
last = 99
counter = 0

Do
     //code inside loop goes here. Always executed at least once.
     counter = counter + 1   //or use counter++
While (counter <= last)      //keeps looping while this is true

Display "The loop ran ", counter, " times."
```

CHAPTER 7: LOOPS    101

Which type of loop should you use? That depends on what the problem requires. As a programmer, you have to figure that kind of thing out. Nobody is going to tell you which loop to use. Through experience and testing, you will know which type of loop to use.

Here are two questions that will help you decide:

> Will the code in the loop be executed at least once?  (that's a post-test loop)
> Can the code in the loop be skipped entirely?   (that's a pre-test loop)

## A Loop with a Sentinel Value

This is a common user-interface design error:

```
Enter number 1: 4
Do you want to enter another number (Y/N)? Y

Enter number 2: -33
Do you want to enter another number (Y/N)? Y

Enter number 3: 209
Do you want to enter another number (Y/N)? No, I hate this!
```

Do you see how annoying that design is? For every number they enter, the user must enter a "Y" to continue.

A better way to do this is to use a *sentinel* value:

```
Enter number 1 (0 to stop): 4
Enter number 2 (0 to stop): -33
Enter number 3 (0 to stop): 0
```

Do you see how much better that is for the user? The word *sentinel,* in this case, means a value that is entered by the user that tells the program to exit the loop. The sentinel value is not used as valid input—it is only used to signal that the user wants to stop entering data.

So, when already asking the user for input, don't ask the user if they want to continue—just look for a sentinel value the user can enter to signal they want to stop. Another example: if the user is entering the names of cities, then let the user enter "quit" to stop.

The next loop we look at will demonstrate how to use a sentinel value in combination with an input loop.

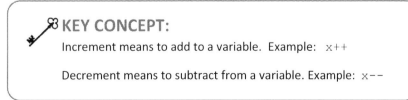

**KEY CONCEPT:**

Increment means to add to a variable.  Example: `x++`

Decrement means to subtract from a variable. Example: `x--`

## An Input While-Loop with a Sentinel Value

A common task for a program is to ask the user to enter a series of numbers or strings such as city names.

The program below uses a priming read and then a pre-test loop to add numbers together. A *priming read* is a statement that gets input before the loop begins.

The program reports the sum of the numbers after the sentinel value is entered. Understanding this loop and being able to reproduce it will save you lots of time. This is a coding tool that MUST be in your toolbox.

```
//Pre-test Loop with input and a sentinel value
Declare Real newValue, sum
Declare Constant Integer SENTINEL = 0

sum = 0                      //Initialize the sum to 0

//The below line is the priming read before the loop
//0 is the sentinel value that will exit the loop
newValue = getReal ("Enter a number. ", SENTINEL, " to exit.")

While (newValue != SENTINEL)  //Continue to loop while true
      sum = sum + newValue

      //other code inside the loop goes here

      newValue = getReal ("Enter a number. ", SENTINEL, " to exit.")
End While

Display "The sum of the numbers is ", sum
```

A key design point is the SENTINEL is a constant and you should write the code so that the SENTINEL value can be changed to anything and the program will still work. This is a constraint that will make you write better code.

Notice the above loop uses a ***priming read*** before entering the loop. This enables the user to enter a sentinel value to end the loop before it even begins. Ending a loop before starting it should be a test case in your test plan.

Why would a user do that? As programmers, we must cover all the possibilities even if they are remote. In this case, perhaps the user realized they were in the wrong program and wanted to exit. Or maybe it was just time for lunch.

> **KEY CONCEPT:**
>
> Infinite loops are loops that never end. Avoid them.
>
> If you start your program and it doesn't seem to be doing anything, it may be executing an infinite loop.

## A wantsToContinue Loop

A common programming task is to ask the user if they want to play again, or if they want to enter another value, or if they want to do it all again. Note that this loop uses the *getYesOrNo(...)* input routine we created in the last chapter.

```
Do

        // code inside the loop goes here

While (getYesOrNo ("Do you want to play again? (y/n)"))
```

Of course, sometimes using a wantsToContinue loop is not appropriate and you should use a loop with a sentinel value instead. Think very hard about using a wantsToContinue loop and consider the user's experience. Consider the wantsToContinue loop as a process that stops the program and restarts it again.

Below is a common error for this type of loop:

```
Declare Boolean wantsToContinue
Do

        // code inside the loop goes here

        wantsToContinue = getYesOrNo ("Play again? (y/n)"))
While (wantsToContinue)
```

Look at the extra lines of code that had to be written. Use the first version.

### A Common Error

Don't write While-loops that loop forever until a condition inside the loop exits the function:

```
Do
        If (this condition is true)
                Return
        End If
While (true)    //This will be an infinite loop if not exited
```

There should be a way to redesign your code to avoid this. Put the condition for leaving the loop in the while statement. If the condition is complicated, use a function that returns true or false.

## For-Loops

Software developers use for-loops all the time. You MUST be so comfortable with for-loops that you can write them without having to think about how to do it.

Here is the format of the For-loop:

*For variableName = startingValue to EndingValue    Step stepValue*

The For-loop has 3 parts:

- Initialize the counter (shown above as variableName) to the starting value
- A condition to continue looping while true. (keep looping until the ending value is reached)
- The amount to increment  (usually +1), or the amount to decrement (usually -1). (The step value)

The *Step Value* can be any increment or decrement. The default Step in pseudocode is *Step +1* if it is not shown.

Here are examples of how for-loops look in pseudocode and in a software language such as Java:

```
For month = 1 to 12 Step 1                        //Pseudocode
for (int month = 1; month <= 12; month++)         //software language

For day = 1 to DAYS_IN_YEAR                        //Pseudocode
for (int day = 1; day <= DAYS_IN_YEAR; day++)     //software language

For eNbr = 0 to nbrOfEmps                          //Pseudocode
for (int eNbr = 0; eNbr < nbrOfEmps ; eNbr++)     //software language

For orcs = nbrOfOrcs to 1 Step -1                  //Pseudocode
for (int orcs = nbrOfOrcs ; orcs > 0; orcs--)     //software language
```

 **KEY CONCEPT:**
Always use integers to loop, never real or decimal numbers.

### A Thinking Exercise:

If programs should always use integers to loop, how would you write a program that needs to loop from 4.0 to 4.1 to 4.2 to 4.3 to 4.4 to 4.5 to 4.6 to 4.7 to 4.8 to 4.9 to 5.0?

This is the type of problem that programmers must solve to be able to solve a bigger problem. Nobody is going to show you how to do it. Think it through!

*Bonus Exercise:*

Write this in a program to demonstrate your solution.

## Nested Loops

Loops of all kinds can be nested inside each other. A very common nested loop is the nested for-loop. How many times does this code display "Hello"?

```
Declare Integer month, year
For year = 2019 to 2028
        For month = 1 to 12
                Display "Hello"
        End For
End For
```

To determine how many times nested loops will execute the code, multiply the number of times each for-loop is executed. The above code will loop through the inner-most code 12 * 10 which is 120 times.

The below code will simulate a clock by moving the various hands.

```
Declare Integer seconds, minutes, hours
For hours = 0 to 23 Step 1
        For minutes = 0 to 59 Step 1
                For seconds = 0 to 59 Step 1
                        // move second hand
                End For
                // move minute hand
        End For
        // move hour hand
End For
```

### Which loop to use?

There is usually a best loop to use to solve the problem.

| Requirement for the program | Try using this type of loop: |
| --- | --- |
| Looping through a defined number of times | for-loop |
| Reading data or getting input | while-loop with a priming read |
| At the end, ask if they want to try again | do-while loop (wantsToContinue) |
| Don't know how many times to loop | do-while loop or while-loop with a sentinel |

## A Game Loop

The below game loop can be modified to play any game that plays any number of rounds. Notice the pattern of the code and how the data moves through each function.

```
Declare Global Constant Integer NBR_OF_ROUNDS  = 5
Declare Global Constant Integer NBR_OF_GAMES   = 3

Main
     Do
          Declare String username
          Declare Boolean playerWins


          username = getString("What is your name?")



          playerWins = playMatch(userName)



          displayFinalResults(playerWins, username)

     While (getYesOrNo("Play again? y/n"))
End Main

Function Boolean playMatch (String uName)

     Declare Integer roundNbr
     Declare Boolean playerWinsRound

     For roundNbr = 1 to NBR_OF_ROUNDS
          playerWinsRound = playRound(username)

          If playerWinsRound
               displayPlayerWonThisRound()
          Else
               displayPlayerLostThisRound()
          End If

          If (insert criteria for player to win match)
               Return True  //The player won the match
          End If
          If (insert criteria for player to lose match)
               Return False //The player lost the match
          End If

     End For

     Return False //No more rounds to play
End Function
```

I
P
O

Notice how similar *playMatch(…)* above and *playRound(…)* below are. This is how great programmers write code so quickly—they are not reinventing code, they are reusing code structures that have already been written.

```
Function Boolean playRound (String uName)

        Declare Integer gameNbr
        Declare Boolean playerWinsGame

        For gameNbr = 1 to NBR_OF_GAMES
                playerWinsGame = playGame(username)

                If playerWinsGame
                        displayPlayerWonThisGame()
                Else
                        displayPlayerLostThisGame()
                End If

                If (insert criteria for player to win round)
                        Return True  //The player won the round
                End If
                If (insert criteria for player to lose round)
                        Return False //The player lost the round
                End If
        End For

        Return False //No more games to play
End Function
```

The result of a game is displayed in the *playRound(…)* function which is one level higher than the *playGame(…)* function. And, similarly, the result of a round is displayed in the *playMatch(…)* function.

At some point, the player has to actually play the game. That point is at the lowest level of the gaming structure: *playGame(…)* in the above example. If you wanted to add more levels to the game, you would keep adding levels of code very similar to the above between *playMatch(…)* and *playGame(…)*.

The details of the above example will change based on the design of the game, but the gaming structure will stay the same. For example, your game may not display anything when the player wins or loses a game or a round.

This is how you can quickly create complicated, layered, programs using coding structures that have already been developed and used by thousands of programmers. Don't try to reinvent the wheel!

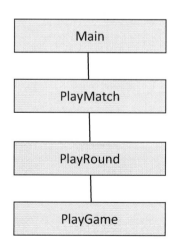

## Removing Code from Main or a Module

It's possible to write small programs so all of the code is in main, but that's not good practice for the larger and more complicated programs you will eventually write. You should strive to remove as much code from main as possible, within reason, and when there is a reason to do so. You should do the same for ALL modules and functions you write.

Ask yourself, can I move any code from main to its own function? Can you move the entire loop and its contents? Or can you leave the loop and move all the code from inside the loop to a function? Can you read the code and tell what it does from the names of the variables, constants, and functions? Below is an example of too much looping code in main. Note that a person would have to read and interpret the code in the Do-While loop to know what the program does.

```
Main
        Declare Integer w, x, y
        Do
                For w = 1 to 10 Step 1
                        Display w
                        For x = 1 to 10 Step 1
                                Display x
                                For y = 1 to 10 Step 1
                                        Display y
                                End If
                        End If
                End If

        While (getYesOrNo("Do it again? y/n"))
    End
```

The above code could be refactored into this:

```
Main
        Do
                displayNumbers()

        While (getYesOrNo("Do it again? y/n"))

    End Main
```

Now my grandmother could read the above code and tell you what it does. She might say something like, "It displays numbers and then asks if you want to do it again." And she would be right.

Good code is self-documenting.

Here is the module being called in the above code:

```
Module displayNumbers()
      Declare Integer w, x, y
      For w = 1 to 10 Step 1
            Display w
            For x = 1 to 10 Step 1
                  Display x
                  For y = 1 to 10 Step 1
                        Display y
                  End If
            End If
      End If
End Module
```

While the above module is good, it could be better by being more flexible. As it is, the *displayNumber(…)* module is restricted to displaying 1 to 10 in all three loops. What if the program needs to loop a different number of times? Here is a better, more generalized, version:

```
Main
      Do
            displayNumbers (10, 10, 10)
      While (getYesOrNo("Again? y/n"))
End Main

Module displayNumbers(Integer outerValue,
                      Integer middleValue,
                      Integer innerValue)

      Declare Integer w, x, y

      For w = 1 to outerValue Step 1

            Display w

            For x = 1 to middleValue Step 1

                  Display x

                  For y = 1 to innerValue Step 1

                        Display y
                  End If
            End If
      End If
End Module
```

Always look for ways to generalize your modules and functions.

## Evolution of Generalized Input Functions:
## Part 3 – Looping when Invalid Data is Entered

As you learn more programming structures and coding techniques in this textbook, we will enhance the generalized input functions that you will be using in your programs. You know how to write functions and you know how to write an if-statement so now we will now use loops to validate the data.

Review and use these generalized input functions:

```
Function String getString (String msg)
      Declare String newValue

      Display msg
      Input newValue

      While newValue is null or spaces
            Display "Error: Missing input."
            Display msg
            Input newValue
      End While

      Return newValue
End Function
```

Notice these are basic input while-loops with a priming read.

```
Function Integer getInteger (String msg)
      Declare Integer newValue

      Display msg
      Input newValue

      While newValue is not an Integer
            Display "Invalid number."
            Display msg
            Input newValue
      End While

      Return newValue
End Function
```

```
Function Real getReal (String msg)
      Declare Real newValue

      Display msg
      Input newValue

      While newValue is not a Real number
            Display "Invalid number."
            Display msg
            Input newValue
      End While

      Return newValue
End Function
```

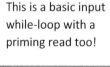

As an exercise, identify the parts of the functions above that are the same and the parts that are different. You don't have to memorize all these functions. Once you understand one, the others follow the same structure.

Study the below code and understand how it works. You will be writing input validation code like this in the next chapter.

```
Function Boolean getYesOrNo (String msg)
      Declare Boolean newValue

      Display msg
      newValue = getString(msg)

      While (uppercase(newValue) != "Y"
         AND uppercase(newValue) != "N")

            Display "Invalid value should be Y or N"
            newValue = getString(msg)

      End While

      If newValue == "Y" Then
            Return true
      End If
      Return false          //newValue is "N"
End Function
```

This is a basic input while-loop with a priming read too!

## Displaying a Shape

When nesting two for-loops, frequently the best way to think of them is looping through rows and columns. Rows are horizontal and columns are vertical.

The below is an exercise to give you practice with for-loops and in thinking about rows and columns. Don't skip this! These are critical thinking skills you need to develop as a software developer.

Here is a shape we want to display in Xs: (think of this shape as containing horizontal rows and vertical columns)

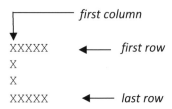

```
                    first column

XXXXX        ←      first row
X
X
XXXXX        ←      last row
```

What is it we want to do here? When do we print an "X"? Say it out loud.

The answer is that if we are working on the first or last row, print "X" in every column. If the row we are working on is not the first or last row, and we are working on the first column, print an "X".

Here is the code:

```
Declare Integer LAST_ROW = 4    //There are 4 rows
Declare Integer LAST_COL = 5    //There are 5 columns

For row = 1 to LAST_ROW Step 1
    For col = 1 to LAST_COL Step 1

        If row == 1 OR row == LAST_ROW
            Display "X"
        Else
            If col == 1
                Display "X"
            End If
        End If

    End For                     //finished all the columns
    Display "\n"                //printing "\n" starts a new line
End For
```

Notice that the code is a translation of the English description of what has to be done. A programmer must be able to verbalize WHAT they are trying to before they can write code to do it.

The "\" in this string: "\n" is an *escape* character. It tells the computer that what follows is an instruction for it to follow—in this case, the "\n" means to start a new line. Another escape code, "\t", means insert a tab.

## Building a Multiplication Table

To demonstrate the thinking process you should go through, and to show how talking about a problem makes writing code so much easier, let's walk through how to print the below multiplication table. First, look at the required output:

```
* |  1  2  3  4  5  6  7  8  9
-----------------------------
1 |  1  2  3  4  5  6  7  8  9
2 |  2  4  6  8 10 12 14 16 18
3 |  3  6  9 12 15 18 21 24 27
4 |  4  8 12 16 20 24 28 32 36
5 |  5 10 15 20 25 30 35 40 45
6 |  6 12 18 24 30 36 42 48 54
7 |  7 14 21 28 35 42 49 56 63
8 |  8 16 24 32 40 48 56 64 72
9 |  9 18 27 36 45 54 63 72 81
```

Can you code this? Give it a try before studying the solution below.

Solution: The output is formatted in 9 rows and 9 columns, so we use row-column nested for-loops like this:

```
For row = 1 to 9 Step 1
    For col = 1 to 9 Step 1

        //Code to be added

    End For
    Display "\n"              //printing "\n" starts a new line
End For
```

Notice there are two header lines:

```
* |  1  2  3  4  5  6  7  8  9
-----------------------------
```

And there are row identifiers:

```
1 |
2 |
3 |   and so on...
```

So where are the 2 header lines printed in relation to everything else?

Think about that before looking at the next page.

The header lines are printed BEFORE everything else. Let's write the code to do that:

```
Display "* | 1  2  3  4  5  6  7  8  9 "
Display "----------------------------- "

For row = 1 to 9 Step 1
      For col = 1 to 9 Step 1
            //Code to be added
      End For
      Display "\n"                     //printing "\n" starts a new line
End For
```

OK, the header lines are done!

Now let's print the row identifiers. Where are they printed in relation to the rest of the multiplication table?

The row identifiers are printed BEFORE the rest of the data for the column, right? OK, find where the column is about to be printed, and let's display the row identifiers before the column's data is displayed:

```
Display "* | 1  2  3  4  5  6  7  8  9 "
Display "----------------------------- "

For row = 1 to 9 Step 1
      Display row, " | "              //row identifier
      For col = 1 to 9 Step 1
            //Code to be added
      End For
      Display "\n"
End For
```

Done!

If you ran the code, this would be printed:

```
* | 1  2  3  4  5  6  7  8  9
-----------------------------
1 |
2 |
3 |
4 |
5 |
6 |
7 |
8 |
9 |
```

So far, so good! Now we just have to code the actual values for the multiplication table. Notice the relationship between rows and columns. Row 1 times column 1 equals 1. Row 9 times column 9 equals 81. That tells us how to write the code:

```
Display "* |  1  2  3  4  5  6  7  8  9 "
Display "--------------------------- "

For row = 1 to 9 Step 1
     Display row, " | "
     For col = 1 to 9 Step 1
          Display " ", row * col          //displays values
     End For
     Display "\n"
End For
```

Run the program and this is displayed:

```
* |  1  2  3  4  5  6  7  8  9
---------------------------
1 | 1 2 3 4 5 6 7 8 9
2 | 2  4  6  8  10 12 14 16 18
3 | 3  6  9  12 15 18 21 24 27
4 | 4  8  12 16 20 24 28 32 36
5 | 5  10 15 20 25 30 35 40 45
6 | 6  12 18 24 30 36 42 48 54
7 | 7  14 21 28 35 42 49 56 63
8 | 8  16 24 32 40 48 56 64 72
9 | 9  18 27 36 45 54 63 72 81
```

Pretty good, but there is one more formatting task to do. The single-digit numbers should be right-justified so the columns line up.

So how would you do that? Think about it before looking at the code on the next page.

Don't give up!

```
Display "* |  1  2  3  4  5  6  7  8  9 "
Display "---------------------------- "

For row = 1 to 9 Step 1
      Display row, " | "
      For col = 1 to 9 Step 1
            If (row * col) < 10
                  Display "  " , row * col //display 2 spaces
            Else
                  Display " ", row * col   //display 1 space
            End If
      End For
      Display "\n"
End For
```

Now everything should print as shown below!

```
* |  1  2  3  4  5  6  7  8  9
----------------------------
1 |  1  2  3  4  5  6  7  8  9
2 |  2  4  6  8 10 12 14 16 18
3 |  3  6  9 12 15 18 21 24 27
4 |  4  8 12 16 20 24 28 32 36
5 |  5 10 15 20 25 30 35 40 45
6 |  6 12 18 24 30 36 42 48 54
7 |  7 14 21 28 35 42 49 56 63
8 |  8 16 24 32 40 48 56 64 72
9 |  9 18 27 36 45 54 63 72 81
```

## Problem Solving

Solving a homework assignment is more than just writing some code. You will have many smaller analysis problems to solve before you even start to write your first line of code.

Decompose the problem (break it down to smaller tasks) and the coding becomes much easier.

Sometimes you may even have to write a small test program to isolate the problem you are encountering and then move the corrected code back into the main program. Professional programmers do not hesitate to write small test programs to save themselves time.

Review the text about *Design and then Code* on page 50. It may be more meaningful to you now.

> Now is a good time to go back and review *Chapter 3: Solving Problems*. The testing and debugging strategies discussed in that chapter will make more sense to you now.

## Review Questions

You should be able to answer these questions, discuss their meaning, and give examples. Pretend you are in a job interview—you should know the answers, right?

1. Name the two basic types of loops.

2. Give one example of one type of loop and two examples of the other.

3. What does increment mean? Decrement?

4. What is a sentinel value?

5. What is an infinite loop?

6. What is a priming read?

7. Describe each line of code for an input loop with a sentinel value.

8. What are the three parts of a for-loop?

9. From memory, describe each line of code in the generalized *getInteger(...)* function.

10. Describe the IPO code in main for a gaming loop.

--------------------

If you are wondering what the teacher wants from your program...

- Refer to the list of **qualities of good code** on page 21.
- Refer to the list of **expectations for the user-interface** on page 26.
- Refer to the list of **internal program expectations** on page 26.

Refer to *Appendix C: Testplan Checklist* and to *Appendix D: Program Checklist* for a structured method of reviewing your program's code.

## Can You Do This?

1.  Code the following in a programming language such as Java, Python, C, C++, or C# and verify it all works by testing it thoroughly. Use a standard *input while-loop with a sentinel value*. The sentinel value of zero must be a constant that could be changed to another value without breaking the program.

    - count the number of even numbers
    - count the number of odd numbers
    - count the number of numbers > 0
    - count the number of numbers < 0
    - sum the numbers

    Send all the counts and the sum to an output module that displays all the counts and the sum. And don't forget to follow the concept of IPO!

2.  First, in pseudocode, so you have to think about it, and then in a programming language such as Java, Python, C, C++, or C#, write nested row/col for-loops to print the below shapes, one at a time. Here are the nested for-loops to get you started:

```
Declare Constant Integer NBR_ROWS = 9
Declare Constant Integer NBR_COLS = 9

For row = 1 to NBR_ROWS Step 1
        For col = 1 to NBR_COLS Step 1
                //Display code goes here
        End For
        Display "\n"                //printing "\n" starts a new line
End For
//and repeat for each shape
```

Think this through and complete the pseudocode before writing one line of code in a programming language.

Too many students consider thinking a waste of time and will try to get this to work using their software language to see if it prints out the correct shape or not. They will try this and try that until it works. That's not writing code—that's wasting their time. People learn to think by thinking. Don't try to use the computer to do your thinking for you.

Here are some shapes to print:

```
XXXXXXXXX
XXXXXXXXX
XXXXXXXXX
XXXXXXXXX
XXXXXXXXX
XXXXXXXXX
XXXXXXXXX
XXXXXXXXX
XXXXXXXXX


XXXXXXXXX
X       X
X       X
X       X
X       X
X       X
X       X
X       X
XXXXXXXXX


X
XX
XXX
XXXX
XXXXX
XXXXXX
XXXXXXX
XXXXXXXX
XXXXXXXXX


        X
       XX
      XXX
     XXXX
    XXXXX
   XXXXXX
  XXXXXXX
 XXXXXXXX
XXXXXXXXX
```

Asking yourself **what** you need to do will help you know what to do to write the necessary code.

The magic of this exercise is that when you describe the solution in English, you will say almost the exact code you need to write. Listen to yourself!

For example:

> For all rows I need to print an X in all columns.

Another example:

> For the first and last row, print an X in all columns.
> For the other rows, print an X only in the first and the last columns, print a space otherwise.

You should be able to write code from that English description of what has to be done!

It might help you to think about these kind of problems by examining the relationship between the rows and columns.

For example, here is how a nested for-loop would print their row and column values:

```
1,1  1,2  1,3  1,4
2,1  2,2  2,3  2,4
3,1  3,2  3,3  3,4
```

So, if you want to print a shape, look at the relationships between the rows and columns and decide when each element should be printed.

What shape would be printed if only elements where the row was >= the column?

```
XXXXXXXX
XXXXXXX
XXXXXXX
XXXXXX
XXXXX
XXXX
XXX
XX
X


XXXXXXXXX
XX        X
X X       X
X  X      X
X    X    X
X      X  X
X       X X
X         XX
XXXXXXXXX
```

3.  Make a shape of your own using Modulus and random numbers!


4.  Code the below enhanced multiplication table in a programming language such as Java, Python, C, C++, or C#.
    Don't look at the pseudocode in this chapter! Ask yourself what you are trying to do and then determine how
    to code that. This is a thinking AND a coding exercise.


```
*  |  1   2   3   4   5   6   7   8   9  |  *
-----------------------------------------
1  |  1   2   3   4   5   6   7   8   9  |  1
2  |  2   4   6   8  10  12  14  16  18  |  2
3  |  3   6   9  12  15  18  21  24  27  |  3
4  |  4   8  12  16  20  24  28  32  36  |  4
5  |  5  10  15  20  25  30  35  40  45  |  5
6  |  6  12  18  24  30  36  42  48  54  |  6
7  |  7  14  21  28  35  42  49  56  63  |  7
8  |  8  16  24  32  40  48  56  64  72  |  8
9  |  9  18  27  36  45  54  63  72  81  |  9
-----------------------------------------
*  |  1   2   3   4   5   6   7   8   9  |  *
```

# Puzzle Time!

```
A  L  G  O  R  I  T  H  M  S  R  O
R  L  O  O  P  D  N  L  A  R  E  U
R  O  S  C  U  M  C  T  T  E  S  T
A  M  P  H  A  U  M  L  E  S  R  P
Y  S  W  H  I  L  E  S  E  G  P  U
I  E  L  S  E  F  M  A  P  K  E  T
T  N  E  A  L  C  O  U  N  T  E  R
S  T  R  I  N  G  D  R  S  A  I  S
A  I  P  O  D  D  U  T  R  L  N  O
B  N  O  B  O  O  L  E  A  N  P  R
R  E  T  U  R  N  U  N  O  T  U  D
R  L  A  C  O  N  S  T  A  N  T  L
```

Circle these words in the puzzle above:

| | | |
|---|---|---|
| ALGORITHM | FOR | OR |
| AND | INPUT | OUTPUT |
| ARRAY | INTEGER | RETURN |
| BOOLEAN | IPO | SENTINEL |
| CONSTANT | LOCAL | STRING |
| COUNTER | LOOP | UML |
| DO | MODULUS | TEST |
| ELSE | NOT | WHILE |

# Chapter 8
# Input Validation

If a program accepts bad input, the output will also be bad—hence the famous phrase: garbage in, garbage out. Many programs consist of mostly input validation, so you need to be able to validate input quickly and effectively without delay to be efficient with your time. Using standard input validation models is critical to be able to write bug-free input validation routines.

**KEY CONCEPT:**
There is a standard model to follow when you need to validate input. You don't need to waste your time reinventing a code structure that has been around for decades.

## Terminology You must Know

As you read this chapter, be sure you learn the definition and reason why the below terms are important. Define and describe each of the below terms out loud. If you can't define a word out loud, you don't really know it! You need to know these terms so you can talk about your code with others.

Input validation          One-function input validation routine
Garbage in                Two-function input validation routine
Garbage out               isInvalid ( variableToEvaluate )

## The Standard Input Validation Models

You have already used the *getInteger(...)* function to validate that the data entered is an integer. That's great, but it's not enough. Most times the program needs a value greater than 0 or another number, or a number that's between two numbers, or a number that's less than another number. The possibilities are endless! The good news is that by following the models presented below, you can quickly and easily create input validation routines that are solid and work without bugs.

The two standard input validation routines are:
1. One-function Input Validation Model
2. Two-function Input Validation Model

## One-function Input Validation Model

The below code uses the standard input while-loop with a priming read and a sentinel. Use the *One-Function Input Validation* model when the input validation condition is simple and does not use more than one AND or OR statement. The below code determines the lowest and highest number entered by the user.

```
Declare Global Constant Integer SENTINEL  = -1
Declare Global Constant Integer LOW_VALUE = 0

Main
      Declare Integer newValue, lowestValue, highestValue
      String message = "Enter number > ", LOW_VALUE, ". ",
                        "Enter ", SENTINEL, " to quit"

      newValue = getValidNumber (message)  //priming read

      If newValue != SENTINEL                 //continues while true
            highestValue = newValue
            lowestValue  = newValue

            While (newValue != SENTINEL)

                  If newValue > highestValue
                        highestValue = newValue
                  End If
                  If newValue < lowestValue
                        lowestValue = newValue
                  End If

                  newValue = getValidNumber(message)

            End While

            Display "Highest value= ", highestValue
            Display "Lowest value = ", lowestValue
      Else
            Display "No numbers entered."

      End If

End Main


//The One-Function Input Validation routine!
Function Integer getValidNumber (String msg)
      Declare Integer newValue
      newValue = getInteger(msg)  //the priming read

      //loop while the input value is invalid
      While newValue < LOW_VALUE AND newValue != SENTINEL
            Display "Invalid Value"
            newValue = getInteger(msg)
      End While

      Return newValue          //returns a good value
End Function
```

Does the code in the getValidNumber(...) function look familiar? It should. This is a basic input while-loop with a priming read just like the code in main! Woo-hoo!

The while loop in getValidNumber(...) continues while the condition is true—in this case, it is true because the data is invalid. The condition should continue when invalid values are found, not valid values.

Can you create a getValidNumber function for Real numbers? Yes, you can.

But what about comparing multiple strings? Or a more complicated numeric requirement? For those kinds of comparisons, use the *Two-function Input Validation* model.

## Two-function Input Validation Model

When the validation condition becomes complicated, use the below two-function input validation model. The function shown below, the getValidNumber(...) model, is good for validating almost anything. Study it and be able to easily reproduce it when you need to validate input—and input could mean data from a user's keyboard, a file being read, a random number function, or even the movement of holographic lightsabers.

The below code counts the number of odd numbers between 10 and 100 entered by the user and displays the count to the user at the end of the program.

```
Main
        Declare Constant Integer LOW  = 10
        Declare Constant Integer HIGH = 100
        Declare Constant Integer SENTINEL = -99

        Declare Integer newValue,

        Declare Integer counter = 0


        String message = "Enter an odd number from ", LOW, "-",
                         HIGH, ", ", SENTINEL, " to quit"

        //priming read
        newValue = getValidNumber(message, LOW, HIGH, SENTINEL)
        While (newValue != SENTINEL)   //continues while true

            counter++

            newValue = getValidNumber(message, LOW, HIGH, SENTINEL)
        End While


        Display counter + " numbers were entered."

    End Main
```

Don't add any other code such as if-statements or while-loops inside the getValidNumber function. Use this coding structure as shown.

```
Function Integer getValidNumber (String msg,
                                 Integer low,
                                 Integer high,
                                 Integer sentinel)
        Declare Integer newValue
        newValue = getInteger(msg)

        //continue looping while the function isInvalid(…) returns true
        While isInvalid(newValue, low, high, sentinel)

                Display "Invalid Value"
                newValue = getInteger(msg)

        End While

        Return newValue            //returns a good value

End Function


//Change this function to meet the program's requirements
Function Boolean isInvalid (Integer newValue, Integer low,
                            Integer high, Integer sentinel)

        If newValue == sentinel
                Return false       // returning false since this is valid
        End If

        If newValue < low
                Return true        // returning true since invalid
        End If

        If newValue > high
                Return true        // returning true to keep looping
        End If

        If newValue MOD 2 = 0   //add as many conditions
                                //   as needed for the problem
                Return true        //in this case 'even' numbers are invalid
        End If

        Return false   //the value of newValue is OK!
End Function
```

Those are the two input validation models to know. You should be able to create similar functions for validating string input by following the sample code above.

Note: The above code confuses some students because the value *True* is being returned when the data is *invalid*. (It is True that the data is invalid). Be sure you understand this code so you can reproduce it easily!

## Validating String Data

To validate String data, you may have to make the inputted value lowercase (or uppercase) and then compare. In some languages, you can use an *ignorecase* function in the comparison instead.

Avoid if-statements like this:

```
If   dataEntry == "Y"   OR dataEntry == "y"
  OR dataEntry == "Yes" OR dataEntry == "yes"
  OR dataEntry == "YES" OR dataEntry == "yeS"
  OR dataEntry == "YeS" OR dataEntry == "yEs"
  OR dataEntry == "N"   OR dataEntry == "n"
  OR dataEntry == "No"  OR dataEntry == "no"
  OR dataEntry == "NO"  OR dataEntry == "nO"
```

That's terrible code.

With a little bit of thought and research into String library functions, you would come up with a better method with fewer lines of code such as this:

```
upperCaseDataEntry = toUpperCase(dataEntry)   //convert to upper case

If   upperCaseDataEntry == "Y"
  OR upperCaseDataEntry == "YE"
  OR upperCaseDataEntry == "YES"
  OR upperCaseDataEntry == "N"
  OR upperCaseDataEntry == "NO"

Then
       //etc.
```

Note: In some languages, like Java, you can't use == to compare Strings.
In Java you have to use the String *equals*() function:

```
if (myString.equals("B")) {
```

**Examples of Common String Library Functions:**

```
theLength = myString.length()

If firstString.equalsToIgnoreCase(secondString)

If firstString.compareTo(secondString)

If firstString.compareToIgnoreCase(secondString)

If firstString.contains("xxx")

If firstString.startsWith("Jan")

myString = myString.trim()
```

## Common Input Values

Data input is a common process that most programs have to do. As a programmer, it's your responsibility to test your code and make sure it works as required.

For String data, test for:

- null (no entry at all)

- space or spaces

- data that does not meet the program's expectations.
  For example, instead of Y or N, the user enters 'abc'

For numeric data, test for:

- null (no entry at all)

- space or spaces

- non-numeric data such as 'abc'

- negative numbers

- zero

- a decimal number such as 3.1415

- a number that is out of range. For example, entering 15 for the number of the month

- a number that is not reasonable for the data.
  For example, entering an age of 3541, or an age of -3

For Yes or No data, test for:

- null (no entry at all)

- space or spaces

- data that does not meet the program's expectations.
  For example, instead of Y or N, the user enters 'abc'

Yes, you must test ALL these conditions for EVERY input! Your users certainly will. Don't assume your code has been written perfectly. ALWAYS test your code to verify you are the genius you think you are.

It's been estimated that 80% of every program is input validation and data scrubbing. If you use the standard input validation routines, you will write better code and finish faster.

**KEY CONCEPT:**

When testing your program, you must test EVERY type of value that could be entered. Don't let your user or your manager find bugs in your program.

A great programmer is a great tester. You have to want to find the bugs in your programs. Only by finding bugs can you fix them and make your program awesome!

## Review Questions

You should be able to answer these questions, discuss their meaning, and give examples. Pretend you are in a job interview—you should know the answers, right?

1.  What is input validation?

2.  Why is input validation important?

3.  Describe each line of the One-function Input Validation Model.

4.  Describe the Two-function Input Validation Model.

5.  Are the loops in the input validation models pre-test or post-test loops?

6.  What is a sentinel value?

7.  When a user is entering Integers, what are three invalid values the program must test for?

8.  When a user is entering a String, what two invalid values should the program test for?

9.  Are there times when you should include the input validation code into another function?

10. What values should be tested when the user is asked this:
    "Please enter an even number greater than zero. Enter -99 to stop."

Review the text about *Design and then Code* on page 50. It may be more meaningful to you now.

> Go back and review *Chapter 3: Solving Problems*. The testing and debugging strategies discussed in that chapter will make more sense to you now.

## Can You Do This?

1. In pseudocode create the following standardized input routines with a loop to display an error message and to ask the user to try again:

   ```
   getInteger (…)
   getString (…)
   getReal (…)
   getYesOrNo (…)
   ```

From now on your programs will use the generalized input routines to get input from the user.

2. In a programming language such as Java, Python, C, C++, or C#, do the following:

   a. In main, create a standard input-sentinel loop for the user to enter the names of months. The sentinel will be the value "q".

   b. Ask the user to enter a month. Create a *Two-function Input Validation* routine for String values. Reject any input values that are not equal to the sentinel value or one of these months: "January" or "February", "March", "April", "May", "June", "July", "August", "September",  "October", "November", or "December".

   c. Use library string function such as ignoreCase(…)  to accept any case for the above words. In other words, the program should accept "jANuarY" and "jANUARY".

   d. If the value is not a correct month, display an error message in the input validation code. If it is correct return the value to main to perform processing and output where the program will tell the user the number of the month. (June is 6, for example).

   Sample Output:

   ```
   * * * * * * * * * * * * * * * * * * * * * * * * * * * * * * * * * * * * *
         My Month Translation Program
   * * * * * * * * * * * * * * * * * * * * * * * * * * * * * * * * * * * * *
   Enter the name of a month such as January (enter q to quit):
   AUGGGGGust
   Invalid Input

   Enter the name of a month such as January (enter q to quit):
   JUnE
   June is the sixth month

   Enter the name of a month such as January (enter q to quit):
   JanuARY
   January is the first month

   Enter the name of a month such as January (enter q to quit):
   q

   Goodbye
   ```

   Note that the displayed month is June and not JUnE.

3.  In a programming language such as Java, Python, C, C++, or C#, do the following:
    a. In main, create a standard input while-loop with a sentinel. The sentinel will be the value -1. Do you know how to code that? If not, go review the input while-loop with sentinel value section on page 102.

    b. Write a *Two-function Input Validation* function that will accept numbers from 10 through 99 inclusive and the sentinel value. Use global constants for -1, 10, and 99.

    c. Add up the numbers and display the total after the user enters the sentinel value.

    d. Be sure to handle the case where the user enters the sentinel value first.

    e. If the user enters the sentinel value as the first value, display "No numbers entered."

    f. Add a do-you-want-to-do-it-again loop around the code in main and start again with the total at zero.

    Here is the sample output:

```
* * * * * * * * * * * * * * * * * * * * * * * * * * * * * * * * * * * *
            My Addition Program
* * * * * * * * * * * * * * * * * * * * * * * * * * * * * * * * * * * *
Enter an even number from 10 to 99 (enter -1 to quit):
0
Invalid Input
Enter an even number from 10 to 99 (enter -1 to quit):
14

Enter an even number from 10 to 99 (enter -1 to quit):
36

Enter an even number from 10 to 99 (enter -1 to quit):
12

Enter an even number from 10 to 99 (enter -1 to quit):
-1


The sum of the numbers is: 62

Do you want to do it again? (y/n) NO

---Program Complete ---
```

You will be writing code very similar to this in your assignments. If you master this now, you will minimize the time it will take to complete your programs later.

# Puzzle Time!

```
Z  B  A  N  D  V  R  E  T  U  R  N
C  O  N  S  T  A  N  T  L  E  U  O
O  B  J  E  C  R  I  P  O  R  A  T
U  M  B  W  H  I  L  E  C  T  R  H
N  M  S  B  P  A  D  L  A  T  R  I
T  M  T  G  L  B  O  O  L  E  A  N
E  O  R  S  V  L  F  O  R  L  Y  T
R  D  I  N  G  E  L  P  E  S  T  E
R  U  N  O  U  T  P  U  T  E  G  G
A  L  G  O  R  I  T  H  M  V  I  E
Z  U  M  L  B  I  N  P  U  T  P  R
T  S  E  N  T  I  N  E  L  F  D  A
```

Circle these words in the puzzle above:

| | | |
|---|---|---|
| ALGORITHM | FOR | OR |
| AND | INPUT | OUTPUT |
| ARRAY | INTEGER | RETURN |
| BOOLEAN | IPO | SENTINEL |
| CONSTANT | LOCAL | STRING |
| COUNTER | LOOP | UML |
| DO | MODULUS | VARIABLE |
| ELSE | NOT | WHILE |

# Chapter 9
# Arrays

Many programs you write will use arrays which is a list of values of the same type. Arrays are useful to hold lists of player names, enemy types, contents of health packs, or lists of employees. Multi-dimensional arrays are useful to simulate locations—either flat (two-dimensions) or in 3D space (in a three-dimensional array). Your program will access each element in an array by its subscript, starting at zero.

To create an array in pseudocode, follow these examples:

```
Declare String  myStringArray  [12]    //this array has 12 elements
Declare Real     myRealArray    [10]
Declare Boolean myBooleanArray [365]
Declare Integer myIntegerArray [99]
```

Here is a graphic representation of a one-dimensional String array called *myArray*:

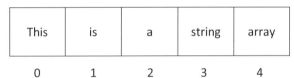

| This | is | a | string | array |
|------|-----|---|--------|-------|

Subscript:    0    1    2    3    4

To access the first *element* in an array use subscript 0 with a bracket like this: myArray[0]. You can use an array element anywhere you have used a variable or a constant in this book. The value of myArray [2] is the word "a".

To set an array element to a value, do the same thing as you would to initialize a variable. For example,

```
myVariable = "my variable"    //You've done this before
myArray [2] = "my"            //Now you can do this
```

Now, after the above line of code is executed, displaying all the values of *myArray* with a space between each element would result in this:

```
This is my string array.
```

The length of the above array is myArray.*length*—which is 5 in this case. The length of the array is 5, but note the subscripts go from 0 to 4. There is no [5] element. The last element in myArray is **myArray [ myArray.length – 1 ]** since the array includes the 0 element.

In many software languages once a basic array is declared to be a certain size it cannot be changed. If you need to expand the array you have to declare a new array, copy the elements from the first array to the second array and then use the second array.

> **KEY CONCEPT:**
> Arrays and for-loops go together like a foot in a shoe, or a hand in a glove, or…
> well, you get the picture.  When you code an array, you will be coding for-loops also.
>
> Much of this chapter will demonstrate using arrays with for-loops.

What happens if you try to access an array with an invalid subscript like this?

```
Declare String myStringArray [9]
myStringArray [99] = "test"
```

The program will crash with an *out-of-bounds error* when the program is executed.

Arrays can be created with 1, 2, 3, or more dimensions, but one and two-dimensional arrays are most common. The code you will read below for one and two-dimensional arrays can be expanded to three or more dimensions very easily. The concepts are the same.

Remember, rather than hard-coding the length of an array in a for-loop or in an if-statement, use *.length* instead. Let the computer calculate the length for you.

## Terminology You must Know

As you read this chapter, be sure you learn the definition and reason why the below terms are important. Define and describe each of the below terms out loud. If you can't define a word out loud, you don't really know it! You need to know these terms so you can talk about your code with others.

| | | | |
|---|---|---|---|
| array | subscript | element | length |
| initialize | search | One-dimensional | Two-dimensional |
| populate | nested | OutOfBoundsError | Off-by-one error |

*"Success in any endeavor requires single-minded attention to detail and total concentration."*

—*Willie Sutton (famous bank robber)*

## One-Dimensional Arrays

A particularly useful function is to find out if a value is in an array by sequentially searching the array using a for-loop and returning *true* if the value is found. Study the below code which populates the array with random numbers between a low and high value and uses the searchArray(…) function to search the array also.

```
Main
      Declare Integer myArray [9]          //creates the array
      Declare Constant Integer low  = 10
      Declare Constant Integer high = 99

      initializeArray(myArray, low, high)

      Declare Boolean valueFound
      Declare Integer nbrToSearchFor

      nbrToSearchFor = getInteger("Number to search for?") //Input

      valueFound = searchArray(myArray, nbrToSearchFor)    //Processing

      displayResult(valueFound)                            //Output
End Main
```

In pseudocode, and in languages such as Java, arrays are passed by reference so this program does not have to return the array. When the values of the array elements are changed in the module or function, the original array's elements are also changed.

```
//Initialize the array with random numbers from low to high
Module initializeArray (Integer [ ] theArray, Integer low,
                                               Integer high)

      Declare Integer x

      For x = 0 to theArray.length - 1  Step 1
            theArray [x] = getRandomNumber(low, high)
      End For

End Module


//Search the array for a value. Return true if found.
Function Boolean searchArray (Integer [ ] theArray,
                              Integer numToSearchFor)
      Declare Integer x

      For x = 0 to theArray.length - 1  Step 1
          If theArray [x] == numToSearchFor
                Return true  //The value was found!
          End If
      End For

      Return False    //The value was not in the array
End Function
```

```
Module displayResult (Boolean vFound)
    If vFound
            Display "The value was found"
    Else
            Display "The value was NOT found"
    End If
End Module
```

```
Function Integer getRandomNumber(Integer low, Integer high)

    Declare Integer randomNbr
    randomNbr = (Math.random() * ((high + 1) - low)) + low;
    Return randomNbr
End Function
```

Or do it this way:

```
Function Integer getRandomNumber(Integer low, Integer high)

    Return (Math.random() * ((high + 1) - low)) +low;
End Function
```

Note that you don't have to reinvent the wheel here. All the code you need to initialize an array and to search an array already exists. You have to understand it well enough to be able to write your own code quickly and efficiently.

Be aware of the *off-by-one error*! Do you see the problem below?

```
Declare Integer myArray [9]

For x = 0 to myArray.length  Step 1
    If myArray [x] = numToSearchFor
            Return true  //The value was found!
    End If
End For
Return false   //The value was NOT found
```

How many elements does the array have? 9. What is the value of myArray.length?  9. But there is no myArray[9] since the numbering starts at [0]. So......Boom! Crash! ArrayOutOfBounds Error!

The for-loop should have been this:

```
For x = 0 to myArray.length - 1     Step 1
```

When you write for loops and arrays, always, always, always double-check your for-loop values.

Mental Exercise:

How would you print an array with commas between each item, but not after the last item like the below list? In other words, how do you not print a comma after the last item?

1, 2, 3, 4, 5, 6, 7, 8, 9

## Two-Dimensional Arrays

A two-dimensional array is a list of items arranged by rows and columns. Look at a spreadsheet—as a programmer you should know how to use a spreadsheet—and look at how the data is arranged: by rows and columns.

When looping through two-dimensional arrays, it is useful to name the variables "r" and "c" for rows and columns.

Check out this pseudocode which uses nested loops to display the subscripts of a two-dimensional array:

```
Module print2DimSubscripts ()
      Declare Integer r, c

      For r = 0 to 3  Step 1
            For c = 0 to 4  Step 1
                  Display r, ",", c, "  "
            End For
            Display  "\n"                  //print a new line
      End For

End Module
```

The subscripts for a two-dimensional array will be printed like this: (row , column)

```
0,0   0,1   0,2   0,3   0,4
1,0   1,1   1,2   1,3   1,4
2,0   2,1   2,2   2,3   2,4
3,0   3,1   3,2   3,3   3,4
```

The above values show the row and column subscripts:  The first item 0,0 is row 0 and column 0. The last item is 3,4 which is row 3 and column 4. The patterns of these subscripts should be in your mind whenever you are coding a two-dimensional array.

Two dimensional arrays are printed as a rectangle or square of values—like a multiplication table.

And you should recognize this code from the printing shapes exercise in the chapter on looping!

**KEY CONCEPT:**

In for-loops use the (array.length - 1) value to end the outer-loop of **rows**. This enables you to change the array length without having to change code related to array size.

For the inner-loop, the **columns**, use the length of the row being processed: array**[r]**.length - 1

Here is code that initializes a 2-D array with random values, sums the values, prints the array, and prints the sum.

```
Main
      Declare Integer myArray [9][9]
      Declare Constant Integer low  = 10
      Declare Constant Integer high = 99

      initializeArray(myArray, low, high)   //Input

      Declare Integer total
      total = sumArray(myArray)               //Processing

      print2DimArray(myArray)                 //Output

      Display "The total of all elements is ", total   //Output
End Main


Module initializeArray (Integer [ ][ ] theArray,
                        Integer low, Integer high)
      Declare Integer r, c

      For r = 0 to theArray.length - 1  Step 1
          For c = 0 to theArray[r].length - 1  Step 1
                theArray [x] = getRandomNumber(low, high)
          End For
      End For
End Module


Function Boolean sumArray (Integer [ ][ ] theArray)
      Declare Integer r, c
      Declare Integer total = 0       //initialize the total

      For r = 0 to theArray.length - 1  Step 1
          For c = 0 to theArray[r].length - 1  Step 1
                total = total + theArray [r][c]
          End For
      End For

      Return total
End Function
```

```
Module print2DimArray (Integer [ ][ ] theArray)
     Declare Integer r, c

     For r = 0 to theArray.length - 1  Step 1
          For c = 0 to theArray[r].length - 1  Step 1
               //print the below with no new line
               Display theArray [r][c], " "
          End For
          Display  "\n"                    //print a new line
     End For

End Module
```

Note that you don't have to waste a lot of time here. All the code you need to initialize an array and to search a two-dimensional array already exists. You just should study it and understand it well enough to be able to write it for yourself quickly and efficiently.

## Initializing an Array with Random Unique Values

How to initialize an array with unique random values should be already clear to you—the program should use the standard input validation model to validate the input BEFORE the random number is added to the array. Study this code:

```
Main

        Declare Global Constant Integer LOW  = 10
        Declare Global Constant Integer HIGH = 99


        Declare Integer [][] theArray = New Integer [5][7]

        initializeArrayWithUniqueRandomValues(theArray)


        //Other code not shown

End Main


Module initializeArrayWithUniqueRandomValues(Integer [][] myArray)

     Declare Integer r, c

     For r = 0 to myArray.length - 1 Step 1

          For c = 0 to myArray[r].length - 1 Step 1

               myArray[r][c] = getValidNumber(myArray)

          End For

     End For

End Module
```

```
Function Integer getValidNumber (Integer [][] myArray)

      Declare Integer newValue

      newValue = getRandomNumber(LOW, HIGH)   //priming read!

      // loop while the function isInvalid(…) returns true
      While isInvalid(myArray, newValue)

            newValue = getRandomNumber(LOW, HIGH)

      End While

      Return newValue

End Function


Function Boolean isInvalid (Integer [][] myArray, Integer valueToCheck)

      For r = 0 to myArray.length - 1 Step 1

            For c = 0 to myArray[r].length - 1 Step 1

                  If valueToCheck == myArray[r][c] Then

                        Return true //it exists so it is invalid

            End For

      End For


      Return false      //it was NOT found in the array

End Function
```

Knowing basic concepts and building blocks will enable you to write code faster and with fewer bugs. You don't have to reinvent the wheel every time you write code.

--------------------

If you are wondering what the teacher wants from your program...

- Refer to the list of **qualities of good code** on page 21.
- Refer to the list of **expectations for the user-interface** on page 26.
- Refer to the list of **internal program expectations** on page 26.

Refer to *Appendix C: Testplan Checklist* and to *Appendix D: Program Checklist* for a structured method of reviewing your program's code.

## Key Array Skills

Being able to process arrays quickly is a key skill all software developers must have. You must know how to do all the following for both one and two-dimensional arrays:

- Initialize the array with values
  - With random numbers
  - With input from the user
  - Use Two-Function Input Validation to prevent duplicate values by searching the array and rejecting duplicate values
- Print the array
  - One-Dim vertically
  - One-Dim horizontally separated with spaces or commas
  - Two-Dim as a rectangle of rows and columns
- Sum the values in an array
  - Add up all the array values
- Find the average value in the array
  - Get the sum of the array and divide by the number of elements
- Find the highest value in the array
  - Set the high value to the first element
- Find the lowest value in the array
  - Set the low value to the first element
- Count the number of even and odd numbers in an array
  - Either create 2 functions or use one and subtract from the count of all
- Search the array for a value
  - Does the value exist?
  - How many times does the value exist?
- Return the index value for a searched value
  - Return the first value found

The good news is all the above functions are similar and, once you learn to do one, the others will become much easier and you will be able to tackle more complicated and interesting problems.

Now would be a good time to go back and review *Chapter 3: Solving Problems*. The testing and debugging strategies discussed in that chapter will be more meaningful to you now.

## Review Questions

You should be able to answer these questions, discuss their meaning, and give examples. Pretend you are in a job interview—you should know the answers, right?

1. What is an array? Give an example.

2. What is a subscript? Give an example.

3. What is an element? Give an example.

4. What is the first subscript value in an array?

5. What is the subscript of the last value in an array?

6. What is an out of bounds error? Give an example.

7. What is an off by one error? Give an example.

8. What does it mean to initialize an array?

9. A Two-Dimensional Array can be thought of as consisting of what? Describe the subscripts.

10. Write or describe each line of a pseudocode function that search an Integer array for a value and returns a Boolean value of true if the value is already in the array. It returns false if the value is not found.

## Can You Do This?

1.  Write a program in a language such as Java, Python, C, C++, or C# that does the below for a one-dimensional integer array. Create a function for each of the below tasks. Return the answer to main and then print the answers in a called output module.

    - Initialize a 10-element one-dimensional array with random unique integer values from 10 to 99
    - Print the array horizontally with a space between the numbers
    - Print a blank line
    - Print the array vertically
    - In main, create a different function to get the value for each of the below:
        o The sum of the values in an array
        o The average value in the array
        o The highest value in the array
        o The lowest value in the array
        o The number of even and odd numbers in an array
    - In a displayOutputReport(...) function, display the values determined above
    - In a standard input-sentinel loop ask the user to enter a value from 10 to 99 (0 to quit) and search the array for the value. Use a standard input validation routine to validate the input.
    - In an output module, display if the number was found or not.
    - Put a do-you-want-to-do-it-again loop around all the code in main to make testing easier.

2.  Write a program in a language such as Java, Python, C, C++, or C# that does the below for a two-dimensional integer array. Create a function for each of the below tasks. Return the answer to main and then print the answers in a called output module.

    - Initialize a 6 by 9 two-dimensional integer array with random unique integer values from 10 to 99
    - Print the array as a rectangle of numbers
    - In main, create a different function to get the value for each of the below:
        o The sum of the values in an array
        o The average value in the array
        o The highest value in the array
        o The lowest value in the array
        o The number of even and odd numbers in an array
    - In a displayOutputReport(...) function, display the values determined above
    - In a standard input-sentinel loop ask the user to enter a value from 10 to 99 (0 to quit) and search the array for the value. Use a standard input validation routine to validate the input. In an output module tell the user if the value was found or not.
    - Put a do-you-want-to-do-it-again loop around all the code in main to make testing easier.

Arrays are difficult to grasp at first, but once you understand them, arrays become easy and fun. It just takes practice!

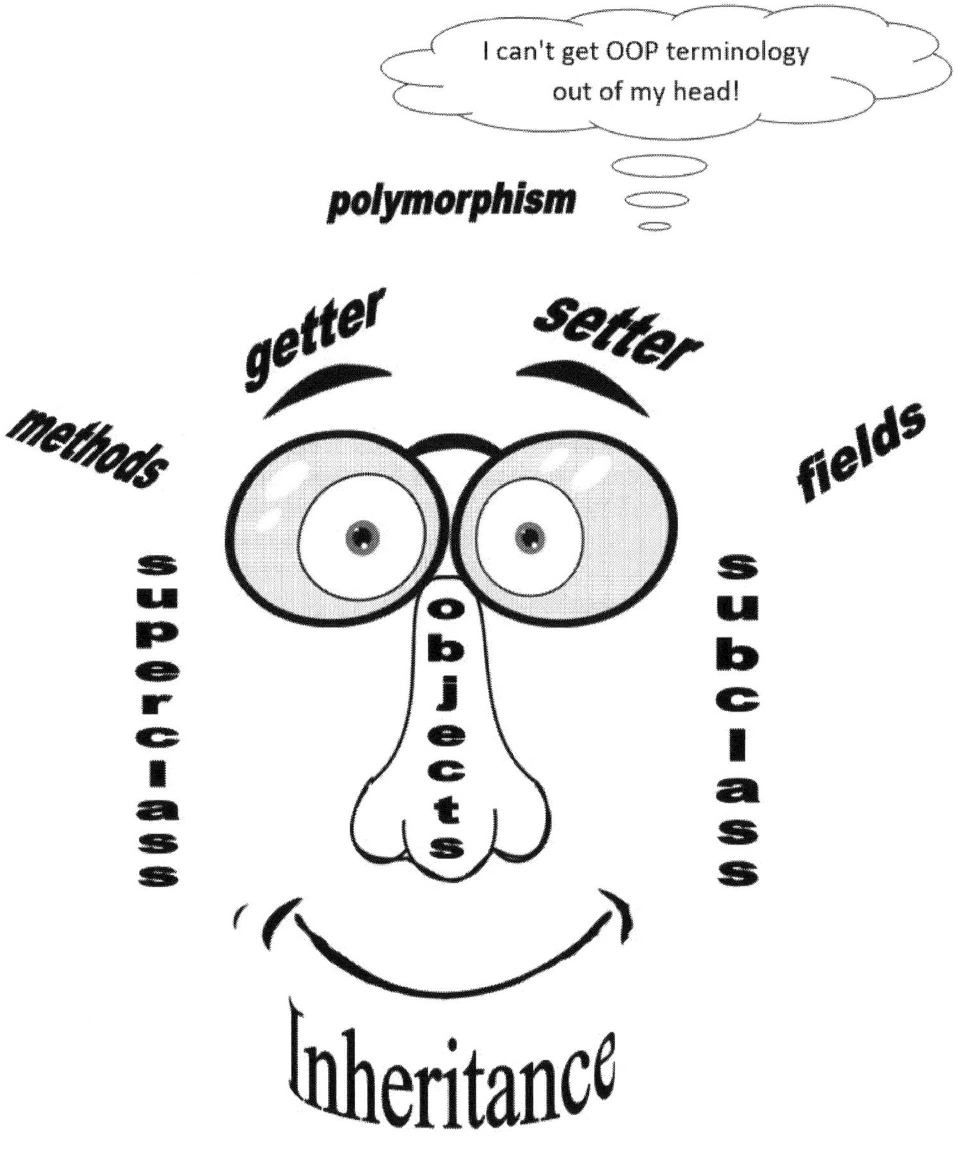
I can't get OOP terminology out of my head!
polymorphism
getter
setter
methods
fields
superclass
objects
subclass
Inheritance

# Chapter 10
# Object-Oriented Programming

So far, we have written code in what is called *procedural* programming—it uses procedures in main, in modules, and in functions—sequentially executing one line at a time. Another method of writing code is called *object-oriented programming* in which the programmer creates objects to mimic the outside world. This chapter is only a brief introduction to OOP concepts and principles.

What are objects? An employee, a hero, a house, a television remote—just about anything you can picture in the real world can be simulated as a software object. Object-Oriented Programming (OOP) is another way of looking at software. But don't worry—we will still use everything you have learned so far in this book in your OOP programs.

## OOP Terminology

Object-Oriented Programming uses all the same concepts you have already learned, but now there are other terms to remember. You must know all of these to talk about and write object oriented code.

| | |
|---|---|
| Class | The blueprint for an object, not the actual object. |
| Object | An object is created from the Class. It contains actual data and methods for the object. |
| Method | Another name for module or function. |
| Getter | A function. A program calls a getter to get the value of a field. |
| Setter | A module. A program calls a setter to set a field to a value. |
| Field | A word OOP uses instead of variable. |
| Private Fields | Variables in a class are set to private so other programs can't update them directly. |
| Public Methods | Methods are public so other programs can use public methods to get or set fields in that program. |
| Constructor | A method named for the class that is automatically run when the object is created. It usually initializes the object's fields. A class/object can have multiple constructors. |
| Encapsulation | Combining data and code into one object. |
| UML | Unified Modeling Language. Like IPO Charts and Hierarchy Charts, UML is used to design object oriented classes and programs. |
| Inheritance | A class can 'extend' another class which allows it to use the data fields and methods in the superclass. |
| Superclass | The general class, such as Dog. A subclass extends a superclass. |

Subclass                The specialized class, such as Beagle. Beagle extends Dog. A subclass extends the
                        superclass.

Polymorphism            An object's ability to take on many forms. An example is on page 159.

## Classes and Objects

The class (file) is the blueprint for creating an actual object. A good analogy is a house's set of blueprints and the actual house itself. You can look at a blueprint (the class), but you can't actually walk into it. You have to build the actual house first (the object, also called an *instance* of the class).

> ### KEY CONCEPT:
>
> Classes and Objects do not run by themselves. They just are. Very Zen.
>
> Objects need to be created and used in a *Driver Program*. The Driver Program does all the work of creating objects, validating input data, telling the object to change its data, printing its data, and more.

Here is some code from a *driver program* that creates a House object:

```
//The below line creates a variable, myHouse, of the type House.
//myHouse has been named, but it doesn't exist yet.
//Note that House is a variable type like String or Integer.
//But it is a variable type YOU created!
Declare House myHouse
```

```
//The below line creates the actual object, myHouse, of the type House.
myHouse = New House( )
```

Now you can do things to *myHouse* like store and change data. You can move in furniture and walk around in it, metaphorically speaking.

```
//The below line creates a variable, myHouse, of the type House
//and it creates the actual object, myHouse, of the type House
//all in one line.
Declare House myHouse = New House( )

//Creating another house object called yourHouse:
Declare House yourHouse = New House( )
```

An *array of objects* can be created like this:

```
Declare Person [ ] people = New Person [10]
```

This doesn't create the Person objects—it creates an array of 10 elements to hold Person objects. A program could create the first object in the array like this:

```
people[0] = New Person( )
```

## Constructors

When an object is created, a method in the class called its *constructor* is executed. Look at this line of code:

```
House myHouse = New House ()
```

See the ( )? That means that is a method, right? That's the *constructor*. A constructor that does not have any arguments is called a no-arg constructor. (No arguments, get it?)

In the House class, you would find this:

```
Class House
        //The No-Arg Constructor
        Public Module House ( )
                //Code that usually initializes data in the object
        End Module
    End Class
```

And check this out: (creating an object with 2 arguments!)

```
myHouse = New House (nbrOfBedrooms, nbrOfBathrooms)
```

See the fields in the "( )"? That means that is a method, right? That's a constructor. And in the House class and object, you would expect to find a constructor that brings in two values as parameters. And you do, as seen below!

```
Class House
        Declare Private Integer numberOfBedrooms
        Declare Private Integer numberOfBathrooms

        //The No-Arg Constructor
        Public Module House ( )
                //Code that usually initializes data in the object
                numberOfBedrooms  = 0
                numberOfBathrooms = 0
        End Module

        //A Constructor accepting two parameters
        Public Module House (Integer bedrooms, Integer bathrooms)
                //Code that usually initializes data in the object
                numberOfBedrooms  = bedrooms
                numberOfBathrooms = bathrooms
        End Module
    End Class
```

Notice in the class above, the data fields are private. That means other programs cannot update the fields directly, but they can use public methods in the class to update the fields' values. This is done for security and to follow the OOP principle of *encapsulation*. The objects created from the class are responsible for the data stored in them. The object has final say about how and when its data can be updated. This is very important for objects that hold money, security clearances, bitcoins, or anything else that should be secure.

## Getters and Setters

In OOP, objects keep their data *private*, which means no other program can directly change the data. Other programs must use *public* methods called *getters* and *setters* to get and set data in the object.

> **KEY CONCEPT:**
> A famous saying you must understand:  Private fields, Public methods
>
> It means just what it says! Fields are private, methods are public!

Notice below that the getter does not need an input parameter, but the setter does. Another program is calling the setter to set a field to something new—so there must be an input parameter.

```
Class House
      Declare Private Integer numberOfBedrooms
      Declare Private Integer numberOfBathrooms

      Public Module House ( )
            //Code that usually initializes data in the object
            numberOfBedrooms  = 0
            numberOfBathrooms = 0
      End Module

      //Getters
      Public String Function getBedrooms ()
            Return numberOfBedrooms
      End Function

      Public String Function getBathrooms ()
            Return numberOfBathrooms
      End Function

      //Setters
      Public Module setBedrooms (Integer nbrBedrooms)
            numberOfBedrooms = nbrBedrooms
      End Module

      Public Module setBathrooms (Integer nbrBathrooms)
            numberOfBathrooms = nbrBathrooms
      End Module

   End Class
```

The below method is also a setter. Because the incoming variable name is the same as the field name in the class, using "this" tells the computer to use the field name for the object instead of the local variable name in the parameter list.

```
Public Module setBedrooms (Integer numberOfBedrooms)
      this.numberOfBedrooms = numberOfBedrooms
End Module
```

**Common mistakes with getters and setters:**

In the below code the local variable *numberOfBedrooms* is set to itself.  This setter needed *.this* as shown above.

```
Public Module setBedrooms (Integer numberOfBedrooms)
      numberOfBedrooms = numberOfBedrooms
End Module
```

In the below two routines the programmer didn't think through what a getter and setter should do. They tried to memorize the form without understanding the function.

```
Public String Function getName (String name)//name not used
      Return userName
End Function

Public Module setName ()
      userName = name        //name is not defined
End Module
```

If you understand what getters and setters are supposed to do, you don't have to memorize so much.

## Inheritance

The concept of inheritance allows a class to extend an existing class. The 'top' class is called the *superclass*. The class that inherits is the *subclass*. The subclass can use any data fields or methods in the superclass without having them in the subclass. This enables the programmer to change code in one place, the superclass, and all the subclasses will effectively change also.

Below is a classic example of inheritance. Beagle inherits characteristics from Dog which inherits characteristics from Animal. Persian inherits data and methods from the Cat class which inherits data and methods from the Animal class.

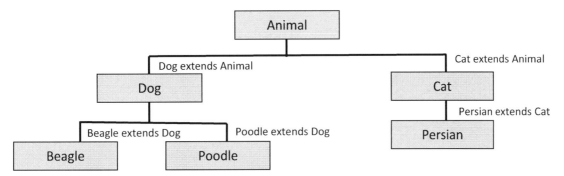

Inheritance can be determined by saying two classes are in an **is-a** relationship. A beagle is-a dog. Therefore, the Beagle class extends the Dog class. A Persian is not a Dog so it does not inherit anything from the Dog class. But a Persian is a Cat which is an Animal, so Persian inherits from Animal.

The Animal, Dog, Beagle, Poodle, Cat, and Persian classes can all be created as objects. Here is how the classes are extended and how a method in Animal can be used in Dog and Beagle objects:

```
Public Class Animal
      Private String name

      //Constructors
      Public Module Animal ()
            name = "undefined"
      End Module

      Public Module Animal (String n)
            name = n
      End Module

      //getters and setters
      Public Module setName(String n)
            name = n
      End Module

      Public Function String getname()
            Return name
      End Function
End Class
```

> If the function *setName()* is not in Beagle, but it is in Dog, the function in Dog will be executed. If the function is not in Dog, but it is in Animal, the function in Animal will be executed.
>
> Note that Beagle does not contain a *name* field, but Animal does. So, because Beagle extends Dog which extends Animal, Beagle does have a name field where his name is stored.

```
Public Class Dog extends Animal
      //Constructors
      Public Module Dog ()
            setName("Undefined in Dog")
      End Module

      Public Module Dog (String name)
            setName(name)
      End Module
End Class
```

> There are two constructors in all three classes.

```
Public Class Beagle extends Dog
      //Constructors
      Public Module Beagle ()
            setName("Undefined in Beagle")
      End Module

      Public Module Beagle (String name)
            setName(name)
      End Module
End Class
```

> In a driver program, here is how objects could be created:
>
> ```
> Animal myAnimal = New Animal ()
> Dog myDog = New Dog()
> Dog yourDog = New Dog("Fido")
> ```

## Overriding a Method

If the superclass and the subclass have a method named the same, the subclass *overrides* the superclass and the computer uses the subclass's method and not the superclass's.

```
Public Class Employee
      Private Integer salary

      //no-arg constructor
      Public Method Employee ()
            salary = 0
      End Method

      //constructor with an argument
      //The "this." Is used to set the instance variable
      Public Method Employee (String salary)
            this.salary = salary
      End Method

      Public Method setSalary (Integer newSalary)
            salary = newSalary
      End Method

      Public Method updateSalary (Integer increment) //overridden!
            salary = salary + increment * 2
      End Method
End Class

Public Class SalariedEmployee extends Employee
      Public Method Employee ()
            //no code. Uses the superclass's constructor
      End Method

      Public Method updateSalary (Integer increment) //this is used!
            salary = salary + increment * 2
      End Method

End Class
```

In OOP, when a SalariedEmployee object is created as shown above, both the SalariedEmployee's constructor and the Employee's constructor are executed.

But, when a program runs the SalariedEmployee's *updateSalary(...)* method, the computer only runs the *updateSalary(...)* method in the SalariedEmployee object. The subclass *overrides* the superclass's method and effectively replaces it. This allows salaried employees to have a different method from the Employee superclass's method.

When a program runs the setSalary(...) method for a SalariedEmployee, the computer sees the method is not in the SalariedEmployee class, so it looks for it in the Employee class. This allows the subclass to *inherit* methods in the superclass without having to duplicate the code in the subclass. That's inheritance!

## Overloading a Method

A program may have two or more methods named the same when they have different parameter lists. You have already seen this when a class contains a no-arg constructor AND a constructor with the same name that accepts at least one parameter.

Overloading is possible for methods other than just constructors too. For example, this is allowed:

```
Main
      Declare Real playerHealth = 0
      playerHealth = calculateHealth()
      playerHealth = calculateHealth(-.1)
      //This is a code snippet. Other code is not shown.
End Main

Function Real calculateHealth ()
      Return (playerHealth * .9)
End Method


Function Real calculateHealth (Real pctToChange)
      Return (playerHealth + (playerHealth * pctToChange))
End Method
```

The computer will know which method to run because the parameter list is different.

Note that the parameter list must be different enough for the computer to tell there is a difference. For example, this will not work:

```
Function Real calculateHealth (Real decreaseAmount)
      Return (playerHealth - decreaseAmount)
End Method


Function Real calculateHealth (Real increaseAmount)
      Return (playerHealth + increaseAmount)
End Method
```

But the below code will work since the computer can distinguish which function to use by the number of parameters or by the sequence of the incoming variable type(s):

```
Function Real calculateHealth (Real decreaseAmount)
      Return (playerHealth - decreaseAmount)
End Method


Function Real calculateHealth (Integer increaseAmount)
      Return (playerHealth + increaseAmount)
End Method


Function Real calculateHealth (Real increaseAmount, Integer bonus)
      Return (playerHealth + increaseAmount + bonus)
End Method
```

## Unified Modeling Language (UML)

The **Unified Modeling Language** is used by analysts and programmers to communicate with each other by using a standard methodology to describe an Object-Oriented group of classes and programs. The top section is the name of the class and therefore the file. The middle section lists the fields. The bottom section lists the methods in the class and the required parameters for each method. A negative sign (-) means private, and a plus sign (+) means public.

The Student class extends the Person class—in other words, Student inherits the fields and methods from the Person class.

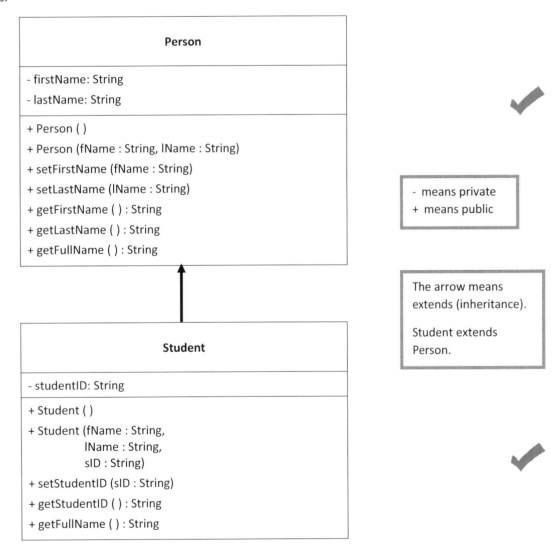

**Person**

- firstName: String
- lastName: String

+ Person ( )
+ Person (fName : String, lName : String)
+ setFirstName (fName : String)
+ setLastName (lName : String)
+ getFirstName ( ) : String
+ getLastName ( ) : String
+ getFullName ( ) : String

- means private
+ means public

The arrow means extends (inheritance).

Student extends Person.

**Student**

- studentID: String

+ Student ( )
+ Student (fName : String,
                lName : String,
                sID : String)
+ setStudentID (sID : String)
+ getStudentID ( ) : String
+ getFullName ( ) : String

## Accessing an Object

Here are two instances of a class being created in a driver program:

```
Person person1 = New Person ( )
Person person2 = New Person ("Janet")
```

Then the driver program can call methods in the object by using the object's variable name, like this:

```
person1.setName("Bob")
name = person2.getName()
```

For more examples, study the code in the next section.


## A Full OOP Example

Using the Person and Student Objects from the prior section, we will need a driver program to create and use the objects.

Here are the specifications for the PersonDriver Program: (what it should do)

1.   Create the first Person object using the constructor with all the parameters
2.   Create the second Person object using the no-arg constructor
3.   Set the first and last name of the second Person object using setters
4.   Display the full names of each Person.
5.   Create the first Student object using the constructor with all the parameters
6.   Create the second Student object using the no-arg constructor
7.   Set the first and last name of the second Student object using setters.
8.   Display the full names of each Student.
9.   Display the full names of each Student which should show the sID also.


Can you imagine the code for each of the above classes and the driver program?

Try to describe the code for each item to someone out loud.


Coding Exercise:

Write the above classes and the driver program in pseudocode.

Compare your code to the code on the following pages.


(If you can't write it in pseudocode, you don't really understand it.)

First, let's create the superclass:

```
public Class Person

    //data fields or properties
    Private String firstName      //note that fields in
    Private String lastName       //  classes are global

    //No-arg constructor
    Public Module Person()
        firstName = "NA"
        lastName  = "NA"
    End Module

    //Another Constructor
    Public Module Person(String fName, String lName)
        firstName = fName
        lastName  = lName
    End Module

    //Setters
    Public Module setFirstName (String fName)
        firstName = fName
    End Module

    Public Module setLastName (String lName)
        lastName = lName
    End Module

    //Getters are functions because they return data
    Public Function String getFirstName()
        Return firstName
    End Function

    Public Function String getLastName()
        Return lastName
    End Function

    Public Function String getFullName()
        Return (firstName, " ", lastName)
    End Function

End Class
```

Next, let's create a subclass that will inherit from the Person superclass:

```
public Class Student extends Person

    //data fields or properties
    Private String studentID

    //No-arg constructor
    Public Module Student(){
        setFirstName("NA")     //Calls the superclass setter
        setLastName("NA")      //Calls the superclass setter
        studentID = "NA"
    End Module

    //Constructor
    Public Module Student(String fName,
                          String lName,
                          String sID)

        setFirstName(fName)   //Calls the superclass setter
        setLastName(lName)    //Calls the superclass setter
        studentID = sID;
    End Module

    //Setters
    Public Module setStudentID (String sID)
        studentID = sID;
    End Module

    //Getters
    Public Function String getStudentID()
        Return studentID;
    End Function

    //This method overrides getFullName() in Person.
    Public String getFullName()
        Return (super.getFullName(), ": ", studentID)
    End Function

End Class
```

Notice that in setFullName() the *super.getFullName()* tells the computer to use the superclass's method. So the Student class uses both its own getFullName() method and the superclass's. The Student class adds the student ID to the full name.

Now, let's create a basic Driver Program that will create 2 person objects and 2 student objects:

```
Public Class PersonDriver
    Public Module Main()

        //Create the first person object p1
        Person p1 = New Person(
                    getString("Enter the first name"),
                    getString("Enter the last name"))

        //Create the second person object p2
        //  using a no-arg constructor
        Person p2 = New Person()

        //Use setters to set data for p2
        p2.setFirstName(getString("Enter the first name"))
        p2.setLastName (getString("Enter the last name"))

        Display p1.getFullName()    //Using a getter for p1
        Display p2.getFullName()    //Using a getter for p2

        //Create the first student object s1
        Student s1 = New Student(
                    getString("Enter the first name"),
                    getString("Enter the last name"),
                    getString("Enter the Student ID"))

        //Create the second student object s2
        //  using a no-arg constructor
        Student s2 = New Student()

        //Use setters to set the data for s2
        s2.setFirstName (getString("Enter the first name"))
        s2.setLastName  (getString("Enter the last name"))
        s2.setStudentID (getString("Enter the Student ID"))

        Display s1.getFullName()    //Using a getter for s1
        Display s2.getFullName()    //Using a getter for s2

    End Module
End Class
```

The above code is all well and good if we have only a few objects to create, but it would become unwieldy if we had hundreds or thousands of objects. How can we organize this better?

With an Array!  (But you knew that.)

```
Program: PersonDriverWithAnArray

Private Person [] people = New Person[4]; //Global array
Public Module main()

    //Create the objects in a loop
    Declare Integer i

    for i = 0 to 1  Step 1    //There are 2 person objects
        people[i] = New Person()

        Display "Person #", i
        //Create the person's fields using setters
        people[i].setFirstName(getString("First name?"))
        people[i].setLastName(getString("Last name?"))
    End For


    for j = 2 to 3  Step 1   //There are 2 Student objects
        people[i] = New Student()

        Display "Student #", i
        //Create the student's fields using setters
        people[i].setFirstName(getString("First name?"))
        people[i].setLastName(getString("Last name?"))
    End For

    Display " "


    //Print all the full names in a loop using a getter
    for i = 0 to people.length - 1  Step 1
        Display people[i].getFullName()
    End For


    //Illustrate polymorphism
    for i = 0 to people.length - 1  Step 1
        displayInfo(people[i])
    End For


End of Module
```

```
//Note the below module accepts Person objects
// but it will also accept any object that
// inherits from Person such as Student: Polymorphism!
Public Module displayInfo(Person p)
      Display p.getFullName()
End Module


End of Program
```

*Polymorphism*. One of my favorite words. Notice above that the *displayInfo*(...) method takes in a Person as a parameter. But the program is sending to it both Person and Student objects. Because Student extends Person the computer will know what to do with each type of object. That's polymorphism!

For the above example to work, the method *getFullName()* must exist in the superclass as well as in the subclasses.

--------------------

If you are wondering what the teacher wants from your program...

- Refer to the list of **qualities of good code** on page 21.
- Refer to the list of **expectations for the user-interface** on page 26.
- Refer to the list of **internal program expectations** on page 26.

Refer to *Appendix C: Testplan Checklist* and to *Appendix D: Program Checklist* for a structured method of reviewing your program's code.

## Review Questions

You should be able to answer these questions, discuss their meaning, and give examples. Pretend you are in a job interview—you should know the answers, right?

1.  What is a class?

2.  What is an object?

3.  What are getters and setters?

4.  What is encapsulation?

5.  What is a constructor and when is it executed?

6.  What is inheritance? Give an example.

7.  What is a superclass? Give an example.

8.  What is a subclass? Give an example.

9.  What is overriding a method? Give an example.

10. What is overloading a method? Give an example.

11. What is UML?

12. What is polymorphism?  Give an example.

## Can You Do This?

From your knowledge of OOP concepts and principles, write the below classes and the driver program.

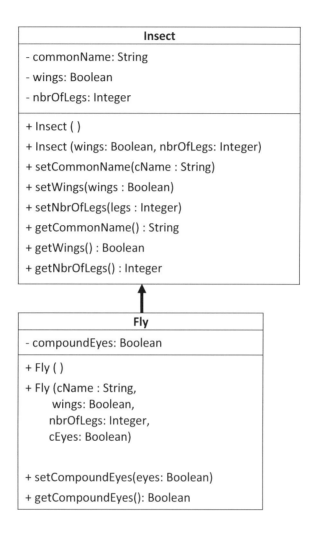

Fly extends Insect.

Specifications for the **InsectDriver** Program:

1. Create the first Insect object using the constructor with all the parameters
2. Create the second Insect object using the no-arg constructor
3. Set the fields of the second Insect object using setters
4. Display the fields of each Insect.
5. Create the first Fly object using the constructor with all the parameters
6. Create the second Fly object using the no-arg constructor
7. Set the fields of the second Fly object using setters.
8. Display the fields of each fly.

"It's not that I'm so smart, it's just that I stay with problems longer."

—Albert Einstein

# Chapter 11
# Solving a Problem Step-by-Step

This chapter walks you through how to solve a larger problem—a problem that is too big to do in your head. The chapter will show one way to solve the problem, but it is not the "right" way. There are many ways to solve a problem and as you gain experience you will be able to choose the best way to solve a specific problem. Even if you follow the below method, with experience you will know when you should do all these steps and when you can skip a step or two.

**The problem:**

Create a program that allows two users to play the common game tic-tac-toe, best of 3 games.
(For this exercise, don't use OOP principles. That will be the next problem for you to solve!)

**Analysis of the problem:**

OK, this shouldn't be too hard since it is in an introductory textbook, right? Let's think about what happens in the game of tic-tac-toe from a programming point of view: get input from each player, validate that input (players can't mark an occupied square, for example), display the board, evaluate the board and tell the players if someone has won. Ties are possible. The program will also have to know if a player has won the first 2 games, so they won't have to play the third.

How will the players enter their moves? This is a console game so everything is done in ASCII text. The shape of the game suggests using a two-dimensional array so that is what we'll use. A player will enter their move by indicating the row and column they want to mark. The program will validate the player's input to make sure the players are entering a proper move. The player will enter row and column like this: 11 through 33. All other values will be rejected.

To think through the possible inputs, let's create a test plan:

| Input Values | Output |
|---|---|
| null (nothing) | Require something to be entered |
| spaces | Require something to be entered |
| ## | Your move must be in 11 through 33 format |
| A | Your move must be in 11 through 33 format |
| 1 | Your move must be in 11 through 33 format |
| A1 | Your move must be in 11 through 33 format |
| 01 | Row values must be 1, 2, or 3 |
| 35 | Column values must be 1, 2, or 3 |
| 11 (and 11 is already filled) | That space is already taken! |
| 11 | Accepted if this space is not already filled |
| 12 | Accepted if this space is not already filled |
| 13 | Accepted if this space is not already filled |
| 21 | Accepted if this space is not already filled |
| 22 | Accepted if this space is not already filled |
| 23 | Accepted if this space is not already filled |
| 31 | Accepted if this space is not already filled |
| 32 | Accepted if this space is not already filled |
| 33 | Accepted if this space is not already filled |

Results:

| | |
|---|---|
| The board is full and neither player won | The game result is a tie |
| A player wins first 2 games | Does not play the 3<sup>rd</sup> game |
| Each player has 1.5 points | Match is a tie |

For both X and O:

| | |
|---|---|
| Can win with top row | Player wins the game |
| Can win with middle row | Player wins the game |
| Can win with bottom row | Player wins the game |
| Can win with left column | Player wins the game |
| Can win with middle column | Player wins the game |
| Can win with right column | Player wins the game |
| Can win with upper-left to lower-right diagonal | Player wins the game |
| Can win with lower-left to upper-right diagonal | Player wins the game |

CHAPTER 11: SOLVING A PROBLEM STEP-BY-STEP

This is a game, so let's use the basic game-loop structure and modify it as needed. The program will also use *getInteger(…)* and *getString(…)* to get input from the players. The program is coming together, and we haven't written one line of code yet.

First, let's design the program output so we'll know what we're aiming for.

```
* * * * * * * * * * * * * * * * * * * * * * * * * * * * * * * * * * * * * * * * * * * * * * * * * * * * *
Welcome to the Amazing game of Best-of-Three Tic-Tac-Toe!

Each player will take turns putting a mark on the board.
Players will enter row and column like this: 12 or 23.
A player will win when they get 3 of their marks in a row.
If the board is filled without 3 in a row, the game is a tie.

The best of 3 games is the winner! Good luck!
* * * * * * * * * * * * * * * * * * * * * * * * * * * * * * * * * * * * * * * * * * * * * * * * * * * * *
----- Game #1 -----
     1   2   3
1:     |   |
    ---+---+---
2:     |   |
    ---+---+---
3:     |   |

What is your move, X? 32

     1   2   3
1:     |   |
    ---+---+---
2:     |   |
    ---+---+---
3:     | X |

What is your move, O? 23

     1   2   3
1:     |   |
    ---+---+---
2:     |   | O
    ---+---+---
3:     | X |
```

And the game repeats until someone wins or the board is filled in. Of course the input could be designed differently by requiring the user to enter: 2,3 or r2 c3 or first the row: 2 and then the column: 3. A good input design can make a game a joy to play and a bad input design make frustrating and unplayable.

Hummm. The program could also determine when 3 in a row is no longer possible to make the game go faster. That is not a stated requirement of the game, but the program should do it anyway. Software developers have to think about possibilities the user never thought of. But, for this exercise, we'll leave that functionality for a later time.

Let's make a Hierarchy chart of the major functions we know we'll need (decomposition!):

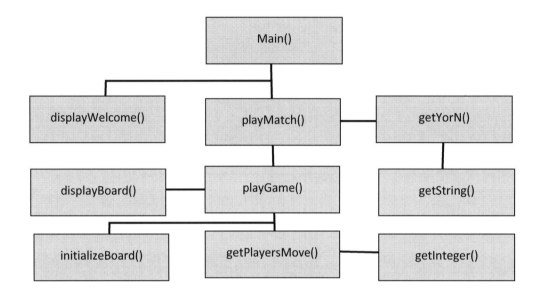

Now let's start by copying in the game-loop code and starting to modify it for our specific game. Since this game can result in a win for either player or a tie, the game-loop will use an integer for the match and game result instead of a Boolean. Every game is different so the basic game-loop will have to be modified accordingly to meet the needs of this specific game. This is pattern recognition and pattern generalization!

The game board is 3x3 so that suggests using a two-dimensional array. Let's define that in main:

```
Declare Boolean gameboard [3][3]
```

No, that won't work. We need 3 values in each element: X, O, and nothing. We could use either integers where 0 is nothing, 1 is X and 2 is O. Or we could use a String array where we put space, X, or O in each element of the array. Let's make it a String array. And in this exercise we'll pass the array by reference so we don't have return the array.

```
Declare String gameboard [3][3]
```

```
Declare Global Constant Integer NBR_OF_GAMES = 3
Main
        Declare String gameboard [3][3]
        Do
                //matchResult: 1=X won, 2=O won, 3=tie
                Declare Integer matchResult
                displayWelcome()

                matchResult = playMatch(gameBoard)

                displayFinalResults(matchResult)

        While (getYesOrNo("Play again? y/n"))
End Main
```

Tic-tac-toe can end a tie so the function *playMatch(...)* returns an integer where 1 means X won the match, and 2 means O won the match and 3 means a tie. Inside the function the players play up to 3 games, but if someone wins the first two games the last game will not be played.

A win will count for 1 point for the winning player, and a tie will count for .5 of a point for each player. Let's display the match score after each game too.

A Mental Exercise:

Think about WHAT has to happen when playing the 3-game match, using 1 means X won a game, and 2 means O won a game and 3 means the players tied the game.

To start out, think about what has to happen without any regard for what order it has to happen in. You can reorder the tasks later.

So, you know you have to play up to 3 games. You know you have to display the match's score. You know you have to display the number of the game they are playing. What else do you have to do to play the game on paper? What do you have to do when a player wins? Or there is a tie?

This is not programming yet. You are thinking about solving the problem first, then you will convert your thoughts to code.

Try to write the steps for *playMatch(...)* before looking at the next page.

Think about it. Grapple with this problem. It is through the struggle that you will learn.

Here is *what* has to be done:

```
Function Integer playMatch (String [][] board)

        //Initialize variables

        //Begin a Loop to play up to 2 or 3 games

                //Display the number of the game they are playing

                //Play the game, returning a result (1, 2, or 3)
                //Display the final board position

                //If X won the game,
                //    add 1 to their score,
                //    and say X won the game

                //If O won the game,
                //    add 1 to their score,
                //    and say O won the game

                //If the game was a tie,
                //    add ½ to their scores,
                //    and say the game was a tie

                //Display the match score: X's points - O's points

                //If X won the match, return 1
                //If O won the match, return 2

        //End Loop

        //All games have been played and nobody won. Return 3

End Function
```

Now we translate the English comments of *what* needs to be done into pseudocode. Can you see how thinking about *what* needs to be done first makes the actual coding much simpler?

A Coding Exercise:
        Convert the above comments to pseudocode.

```
Function Integer playMatch (String [][] board)

      Declare Integer result //1=X won, 2=O won, 3=tie
      Declare Integer gameNbr
      Declare Real xScore, oScore
      xScore = 0
      oScore = 0

      For gameNbr = 1 to NBR_OF_GAMES
            Display "----- Game number ", gameNbr, " -----"

            //result of: 1=X won, 2=O won, 3=tie
            result = playGame(board)

            displayBoard(board)
            If (result == 1)
                  xScore++
                  Display "X won this game!"
            Else If (result == 2)
                  oScore++
                  Display "O won this game!"
            Else
                  xScore = xScore + .5
                  oScore = oScore + .5
                  Display "Nobody won this game. Tie!"
            End If

            Display "The score is: ", xScore, "-", oScore

            If (xScore > (NBR_OF_GAMES * .5))
                  Return 1        //X won the match
            End If
            If (oScore > (NBR_OF_GAMES * .5))
                  Return 2        //O won the match
            End If
      End For
      Return 3   //tie!
End Function
```

Notice the line of code from above:

```
      If (xScore > NBR_OF_GAMES * .5))
```

I could have wrote it like this:

```
      If (xScore > 1.5))
```

But that restricts the code to a 3-game match (1/2 of 3 is 1.5). Now the code allows a match of 5, 7, or more games. Always try to make your code flexible and not tied to specific values in the problem statement.

We can add the below modules and generalized input functions before we do anything else.

**Module displayWelcome()**
```
    Display "******************************************************"
    Display "Welcome to the Amazing game of Best-of-Three Tic-Tac-Toe!"
    Display ""
    Display "Each player will take turns putting a mark on the board. "
    Display "Players will enter row and column like this: 12 or 23."
    Display "A player will win when they get 3 of their marks in a row. "
    Display "If the board is filled without 3 in a row, the game is a tie."
    Display ""
    Display "The best of 3 games is the winner! Good luck! "
    Display "******************************************************"
```
**End Module**

**Function displayFinalResults (Integer result)**
```
    If result == 1
        Display "X won the match!)
    Else if result == 2
        Display "O won the match!)
    Else
        Display "The match is a tie!"
    End If
```
**End Function**

**Function String getString (String msg)**
```
    Declare String newValue

    Display msg
    Input newValue

    While newValue is null or spaces
        Display "Error: Missing input."
        Display msg
        Input newValue
    End While

    Return newValue
```
**End Function**

```
Function Integer getInteger (String msg)
      Declare Integer newValue

      Display msg
      Input newValue

      While newValue is not an Integer
            Display "Error: Invalid number."
            Display msg
            Input newValue
      End While

      Return newValue
End Function


Function Boolean getYesOrNo (String msg)
      Declare Boolean newValue

      Display msg
      newValue = getString(msg)

      While (uppercase(newValue) != "Y"
         AND uppercase(newValue) != "N")

            Display "Invalid value should be Y or N"
            newValue = getString(msg)

      End While

      If newValue == "Y" Then
            Return true
      End If
      Return false
End Function
```

There! We have a lot of code done and we haven't even tackled the game code yet. Now we have to start to get very specific for our game.

Let's initialize our two-Dim array to spaces—which we know how to do already, right?

```
Function initializeBoard (String [][] board)
      Declare Integer r, c
      For r = 0 to 2 Step 1
            For c = 0 to 2 Step 2
                  board [r][c] = " "
            End For
      End For
      Return board
End Function
```

Now let's print the board so we can see the input values once they are entered. We could try to modify the standard print of a two-dimensional array with the extra board elements, but since we know this is a 3x3 board, let's code it for our specific game...

```
Module displayBoard (String [ ][ ] theBoard)
      Display "    1    2    3"
      Display "1:  ", theBoard [0][0],
            " | ", theBoard [0][1],
            " | ", theBoard [0][2]
      Display "   ---+---+---"
      Display "2:  ", theBoard [1][0],
            " | ", theBoard [1][1],
            " | ", theBoard [1][2]
      Display "   ---+---+---"
      Display "3:  ", theBoard [2][0],
            " | ", theBoard [2][1],
            " | ", theBoard [2][2]
End Module
```

If we ran the above module, we should see a blank board with lines showing the squares.

Playing the game may be the most complicated thing we have to do, so let's do the input validation first. Because this is a more complicated input validation, we'll use a *Two-Function Input Validation* structure. Let's copy that code and modify it for our specific String input values.

```
Function Integer getPlayersMove (String msg, String [][] board)

        Declare Integer newValue
        newValue = getInteger(msg)

        // loop while the function isInvalid(…) returns true
        While (isInvalid(newValue, board))
              //Not displaying a general error message here.
              newValue = getInteger(msg)
        End While

        Return newValue

End Function
```

A Coding Exercise:

Write the *isInvalid(…)* function in pseudocode before comparing your code to the code on the next page.

First, think about WHAT the routine has to do. What are the invalid values? What is valid? Your test plan will already hold the answers to those questions.

So how do you verify the first digit is 1, 2, or 3? How do you verify the second digit is 1, 2, or 3? This is math that you have to know: divide a number by 10 to strip off the one's place. Use modulus to get the one's value.

In your job, you will be expected to solve problems like this. You won't be able to Google the answer or ask someone else. You will be expected to think about it, struggle with it, and eventually solve it.

You can do it if you don't give up!

First, let's check for the proper length of the input value. Since the player is entering an integer that represents rows and columns, the valid values are: 11, 12, 13, 21, 22, 23, 31, 32, 33. Since there are only 9 possible values, we could hard code them in an if-statement, but a good computer scientist wouldn't even consider doing that.

Look at the values. Our first check can be for values between 11 and 33. If our design required the player to enter a string such as r1c2, we would first validate the length of the string using String library functions before looking at the content of the string.

```
Function Boolean isInvalid (Integer newValue, String [][] board)

    If (newValue < 11 OR newValue > 33)
         Display "Your move must be in 11 through 33 format"
         Return true  //this is a bad value
    End If

    /*This code is not necessary since we already checked for 11 to 33
    If  (((newValue / 10) != 1)       //this gets the 10s digit
     AND ((newValue / 10) != 2)
     AND ((newValue / 10) != 3))
    Then
         Display "Row values must be 1, 2, or 3"
         Return true  //this is a bad value
    End If
    */

    If  (((newValue MOD 10) != 1)     //this gets the rightmost ones digit
     AND ((newValue MOD 10) != 2)
     AND ((newValue MOD 10) != 3))
    Then
         Display "Column values must be 1, 2, or 3"
         Return true  //this is a bad value
    End If

    //See if the board already has an X or an O in that space
    //Subtract one from the player's entry to get the array subscript
    If (board [(newValue / 10) - 1]
            [(newValue MOD 10) - 1] != " ")
         Display "That space is already taken!"
         Return true  //this is an error
    End If

    Return false      // the value of newValue is OK!
End Function
```

So far, so good. We have a lot of code and now I would test the *getValidMove(...)* function at this point to verify the code works as I expect it to. Once this is tested, I don't have to think about it again.

Now we're ready to tackle the crux of the problem: playing the actual game. As I write the below code I keep thinking about WHAT has to happen when 2 people play tic-tac-toe: player x makes a move and puts it on the board, check for a win or tie, then player O makes a move and puts it on the board, and check for a win or a tie. And repeat. Once I can say what I want to happen in English, then I can translate my answer from the English language to a software language.

Here are the steps I came up with to play the game in English.

```
Function Integer playGame (String [][] theBoard)

        //clear the Board for a new game

        //Begin a Loop
                //Display the Board
                //Ask player X to enter their move
                //Get Player X's Move
                //Put the move on the board
                //check for a win or a tie

                //If X did not win and it's not a tie,continue playing
                        //Display the Board
                        //Ask player O to enter their move
                        //Get Player O's Move
                        //Put the move on the board
                        //check for a win or a tie
                //End If

        //Continue Looping while the game continues
        //The match is a tie: they played 3 games and nobody won
End Function
```

Of course, several of the above statements that use verbs such as: get... and check... will be functions that will return a value to the *playGame(...)* routine. The Display statement will be a module without a returning value.

The "Ask the Player" and "get the player's move" lines above will be combined into the *getPlayersMove(...)* function we already wrote.

The "check for a win or tie" lines will result in a return statement leaving the *playGame(...)* function.

And remember that the players are entering locations from 11 to 33, but the actual array subscripts are 00 to 22. So, the program has to subtract 1 from the player's entry to get the array subscript value to update the board. Let's convert the English to code, but leave the checking for a win or tie until later.

```
Function Integer playGame (String [][] theBoard )
      Declare Integer move
      Declare result = 0

      initializeBoard()

      Do
            //It is X's turn
            displayBoard(theBoard)

            move = getPlayersMove ("What is your move, X?")

            board [(move / 10) - 1][(move MOD 10) - 1] = "X"

            //TO DO: check for a win or a tie here,
            //        returning a result

            If (result == 0)              //0=continue playing
                  //It is O's turn
                  displayBoard(theBoard)

                  move = getPlayersMove ("What is your move, O?")

                  board [(move / 10) - 1][(move MOD 10) - 1] = "O"

                  //TO DO: check for a win or a tie here,
                  //        returning a result
            End If

      While (result == 0)    //0=continue playing

      Return 3               //tie
End Function
```

Now I can compile and run this code and the game should be playable, but without anybody winning yet. But I can test that my input validation is working correctly and that the entered moves are put in the proper places in the board array. That's a lot. We're making great progress!

Actually, I'm not thrilled with the duplicate code in this function, but it works. I'll leave this refactoring to you to do!

Now let's check for a win or a tie. Since we are doing that twice, once for each player, that code should be in a function so we don't repeat code.

A Mental Exercise:

> What has to be done to check for a win? Don't think about code. Think about the game itself. Every grade-schooler knows how to win a game of tic-tac-toe.

Did you think about it? Here is the function to determine if someone won a game of tic-tac-toe.

```
Function Integer checkForWin (String [][] board)

        //For X and for O:
        //    3-in-a-line on the top row
        //    3-in-a-line on the middle row
        //    3-in-a-line on the bottom row
        //    3-in-a-line on the first column
        //    3-in-a-line on the second column
        //    3-in-a-line on the third column
        //    3-in-a-line on the upper left to lower right diagonal
        //    3-in-a-line on the lower left to upper right diagonal
        //If none of those are true, the game continues
        //until the board is full, which is a tie.

End Function
```

So that's what we have to code. Now we just have to translate ENGLISH to code.

Another reminder: If you can't say WHAT you need to do in English, you can't write it in code!

```
//0=nobody won, 1=X won, 2=O won, 3=board is full so it's a tie
Function Integer checkForWin (String [][] board)

        //    3-in-a-line on the top row
        If    board [0][0] == "X"
         AND board [0][1] == "X"
         AND board [0][2] == "X"
        Then
                Return 1  //X has won
        End If

        If    board [0][0] == "O"
         AND board [0][1] == "O"
         AND board [0][2] == "O"
        Then
                Return 2  //O has won
        End If

        //code to be added for each row, the 3 columns,
        // and the 2 diagonals for both X and O

End Function
```

Wait a minute! There appears to be duplicate code again. Arrays and for-loops go together so let's put all that code into a loop.

```
//0=nobody has won, 1=X won, 2=0 won, 3=board is full so it's a tie
Function Integer checkForWin (String [][] board)

    Declare Integer r, c

    //Check for horizontal 3-in-a-line first, all rows
    For r = 0 to 2 Step 1

        If ((board [r][0] == "X")
        AND (board [r][1] == "X")
        AND (board [r][2] == "X"))
        Then
            Return 1  //X has won
        End If

        If  ((board [r][0] == "O")
         AND (board [r][1] == "O")
         AND (board [r][2] == "O"))
        Then
            Return 2  //O has won
        End If
    End For

    //Check for vertical 3-in-a-line next
    For c = 0 to 2 Step 1
        If  ((board [0][c] == "X")
         AND (board [1][c] == "X")
         AND (board [2][c] == "X"))
        Then
            Return 1  //X has won
        End If

        If  ((board [0][c] == "O")
         AND (board [1][c] == "O")
         AND (board [2][c] == "O"))
        Then
            Return 2  //O has won
        End If
    End For
```

```
//Check for left to right down diagonal 3-in-a-line next
If  ((board [0][0] == "X")
 AND (board [1][1] == "X")
 AND (board [2][2] == "X"))
Then
     Return 1  //X has won
End If

If  ((board [0][0] == "O")
 AND (board [1][1] == "O")
 AND (board [2][2] == "O"))
Then
     Return 2  //O has won
End If

//Check for left to right up diagonal 3-in-a-line next
If  ((board [0][2] == "X")
 AND (board [1][1] == "X")
 AND (board [2][0] == "X"))
Then
     Return 1  //X has won
End If

If  ((board [0][2] == "O")
 AND (board [1][1] == "O")
 AND (board [2][0] == "O")
Then
     Return 2  //O has won
End If

//Check for a full board
If (isBoardFull(board))
Then
      Return 3
End If

//Future TO DO: Check to see if anyone can win now at all

Return 0   //The game continues
```
**End Function**

Hold on! There appears to be duplicate code again. The above code does the same thing for X and for O. Time to generalize a function! Let's pass in "X" or "O" to the function and get rid of the duplicate code.

Coding Exercise:

Code the above passing (String player) into the function to eliminate duplicate code.

```
//0=nobody has won, 1=a player won, 3=board is full so it's a tie
Function Integer checkForWin (String player, String [][] board)

    Declare Integer r, c

    //Check for horizontal 3-in-a-line first, all rows
    For r = 0 to 2 Step 1
        If ((board [r][0] == player)
        AND (board [r][1] == player)
        AND (board [r][2] == player))
        Then
            Return 1  //a player has won
        End If
    End For

    //Check for vertical 3-in-a-line next
    For c = 0 to 2 Step 1
        If  ((board [0][c] == player)
         AND (board [1][c] == player)
         AND (board [2][c] == player))
        Then
           Return 1  //a player has won
        End If
    End For

    //Check for left to right down diagonal 3-in-a-line next
    If  ((board [0][0] == player)
     AND (board [1][1] == player)
     AND (board [2][2] == player))
    Then
        Return 1     //a player has won
    End If

    //Check for left to right up diagonal 3-in-a-line next
    If  ((board [0][2] == player)
     AND (board [1][1] == player)
     AND (board [2][0] == player))
    Then
        Return 1     //a player has won
    End If

    //Check for a full board
    If (isBoardFull(board))
    Then
        Return 3   //The board is full, so the game is a tie
    End If

    Return 0          //The game continues
End Function
```

```
Function Boolean isBoardFull (String [][] theBoard)
    For r = 0 to 2 Step 1
        For c = 0 to 2 Step 1
            If (theBoard [r][c] == " ")
            Then
                Return false  //at least one blank space
            End If
        End For
    End For

    Return true   //No blank spaces were found
End Function
```

Now we have to modify the *playGame(…)* routine to use the new functions we just created and to return the proper value to *playMatch*.

```
Function Integer playGame (String [][] theBoard )
    Declare Integer move
    Declare Integer result = 0

    initializeBoard()

    Do
        //It is X's turn
        displayBoard(theBoard)

        move = getPlayersMove ("What is your move, X?", theBoard)

        theBoard [(move / 10) - 1] [(move MOD 10) - 1] = "X";

        result = checkForWin(theBoard)

        if (result == 0)                  //0=continue playing
            //It is O's turn
            displayBoard(theBoard)

            move = getPlayersMove ("What is your move, O?",
                                                theBoard)

            theBoard [(move / 10) - 1]
                    [(move MOD 10) - 1] = "O";

            result = checkForWin(theBoard)
            if (result == 1)
                result = 2    //O won
            End If
        End If

    While (result == 0)       //0=continue playing

    Return result             //return: 1=X won, 2=O won, 3=tie
End Function
```

And we are done with initial coding. Now we have to compile and test ALL the test cases in our test plan and then play it many times to give us confidence it works as we want it to.

Can you see how difficult it would have been to keep all that in your head as you coded it? Once you start writing more complicated programs it is imperative that you use a well-structured method to analyze, write your code, and test. A random, give-this-a-try method just won't cut it. You will waste a lot of time if you don't approach solving the problem in an organized manner.

Is the above method the only way to write a tic-tac-toe game? Of course not. This chapter is merely intended to show you one way to think about and code a more complicated program.

What else could be done with this tic-tac-toe program? Lots!

- Make "X" and "O" global constants.
- Make global constants for TIE, X_WINS, and Y_WINS instead of explicitly using 0, 1 and 2.
- Let the players enter their own values instead of using X and O.
- Stop the game early when 3-in-a-line is no longer possible.
- Randomly decide who starts the game so X or O does not start first every time.
- Let the user select any size board from any size rows and columns from 3x3 to 9x9 and change the winning condition accordingly.
- Code the game using OOP principles (!).
- Make one of the players an Artificial Intelligence that plays against the human and never loses.
- Make this a three-dimensional game: 3x3x3
- Play until the entire board if full and assign points for 2 in a row, 3 in a row, etc. The player with the high score wins.

I hope this peek into my thought process will help you think through your own programs. Best wishes for delivering bug-free code! (after a lot of testing and fixing of your program's bugs, of course).

## Can You Do This?

Take the code for the tic-tac-toe game and write it in a programming language such as Java, Python, C, C++, or C#. Test it thoroughly. Have fun!

# Appendix A: Index and Glossary

These terms are used in this textbook. You should know what all these terms mean. Yes, all of them.

| Term | Definition or Description | Page Number |
|---|---|---|
| algorithm | A sequence of instructions. Like a recipe for cooking a cake, algorithms tell the computer exactly the steps to take to solve the problem. | 23 |
| AND | A Logical operator used to combine conditions. | 78 - 81 |
| arguments | A list of variables being passed to a module or function. See *parameters*. | 55 - 56 |
| array | A list of values, referenced by their subscript. | 133 – 141 |
| array of objects | An array of objects can be created like this: Declare Person [ ] people = New Person [10] | 146 |
| Boolean values | The values True or False. | 78, 80, 81 |
| boundary conditions | Values used to test a program that are mentioned in the problem statement or are 1 above or 1 below the mentioned values. | 36 |
| Break | Used in a Select statement to go to the end of the Select statement's block of code. | 87 |
| calling statement | The statement used to start a function. After the function ends, control of the program returns to the calling statement. | 53 – 55 |
| camelCase | In this textbook, variables are named using the camelCase naming standard. The first letter of each word is capitalized. Example: myFirstVariable | 40, 57 |
| case | 1. UPPER or lower case. | 40 |
| | 2. Used in the Select statement to determine which lines of code will be executed. | 87 |
| class | The blueprint for an object. This is a blueprint, not the actual object. | 145, 146 |

| | | |
|---|---|---|
| common test values | Values that are entered by the user when using the program. | 128 |
| comparing strings | Strings can be compared like numbers. | 84, 127 |
| computational thinking | Thought processes involved in understanding a problem and expressing a solution in such a way that a human and computer can effectively carry it out. | 22 |
| constant | A value that does not change during the running of the program. Constants are named in UPPER_CASE with an underscore between words. | 40 – 42 |
| constructor | A method named for the class that is automatically run when the object is created. It usually just initializes data. A class/object can have multiple constructors | 147 |
| counter | A variable used to count the number of occurrences of an item. Example: counter++ | 100 |
| counting loop | A loop used to count the number of items either being entered or already in an array. | 100 |
| debugging | Testing a program, looking for bugs. | 33-34 |
| decomposition | Breaking down a complex problem into smaller and easier to solve problems. This is a basic problem solving skill. | 22, 54 |
| decrement | To reduce. Example of x minus one: x-- | 44, 101 |
| default | In a select statement the default case is used when none of the case statements are used. | 87 |
| Display | Used to show values on the screen. | 42 |
| Do-While-loop | A post-test loop. Do *these-lines-of-code* while *this-is-true*. | 99, 100 |
| driver program | A program used to create and process objects. | 146, 154 |
| element | One part of an array. Starts at 0. Example: myArray [0] | 133, 134 |
| Else | Part of a conditional If-statement. If this-is-true *do-these-lines-of-code* Else *do-these-instead*. | 79 |
| encapsulation | Combining data and code into one object | 145, 147 |
| escape character | A character in an string to tell the computer not print this, but to do something. Examples: "\n" and "\t" | 112 |

| | | |
|---|---|---|
| expectations | Users have expectations and programs also have expectations. Good programmers meet those expectations. | 26 |
| field | A word OOP uses instead of variable | 145, 147, 149 |
| Formulas | Mathematical expressions whose result is put into a variable. | 44 |
| For-loop | A pre-test loop consisting of 3 parts: initialize the counter; test the counter; increment the counter. | 99, 104, 105, 108, 109 |
| Function | A group of code that returns a value to the calling statement. | 53 |
| Function header | The first line of a group of lines of code that returns a value to the calling statement. | 56 |
| game loop | A loop frequently used in games. | 106 |
| garbage in | Garbage is bad input that programs should reject. | 123 |
| garbage out | If bad input is allowed in a program, the result will be bad also. | 123 |
| generalized input validation routines | Generalized functions that get input from the user. | 73, 90, 110 |
| generalized modules and functions | Modules and functions that can be used for a variety of purposes. | 70 |
| getter | A function. A program calls a getter to get the value of a field | 145, 148 |
| global constant | A constant known to the entire program must be declared globally. OK to use because they do not change. | 54, 59 |
| global variable | A variable known to the entire program must be declared globally. Do not create global variables unless approved by your teacher or manager. Global variables make debugging difficult. | 59 |
| Hierarchy Chart | A chart of modules and functions in a program. Used for design and for documentation. | 65 |
| highest value | In an input-loop, programs can find the highest value entered. | 124 |
| If | A conditional statement. If *this-is-true*, execute these lines of code. | 77-86 |
| increment | To increase the value of a variable. Example: x++ | 44, 101 |
| infinite loop | A loop that never ends. This is not good. | 103 |

| | | |
|---|---|---|
| inheritance | A class can 'extend' another class which allows it to use the data fields and methods in the superclass. | 145, 146, 149, 150 |
| initialization | Setting a variable or the elements of an array to a value. | 40 |
| initialize | Setting a variable or the elements of an array to a value. | 40 |
| Input | Used to get data from the user. The result is put into a variable. Example: Input username | 43 |
| input validation | A process where the program verifies the user entered valid values. If not, the data is rejected. | 90, 123-128 |
| instance | The object created from a Class. An instance of a Class. | 146, 147, 149 |
| Integer | A whole number such as: -4, 0, 2, 28 | 40, 42 |
| Integer variable type | Used when declaring an integer number. Example: Declare Integer myIntegerNumber = 0 | 40, 42 |
| IPO | Input-Processing-Output. The sequence of tasks in a well-structured program. | 45 |
| IPO Chart | Short for Input-Processing-Output chart. Used to document what a function should do. | 45, 66, 97 |
| isInvalid(variable) | The second function in the Two-Function Input Validation model. Returns true when the value is invalid. | 126, 140, 173 |
| length | Variables and Arrays have a length. Array length is commonly used in for-loops. | 137 |
| local scope | The scope of a variable or constant. Local scope is limited to the function where the variable or constant is declared. | 54, 59 |
| local constant | A local constant is declared in a function and is only known in that function. Its scope is local. | 59 |
| local variable | A local variable is declared in a function and is only known in that function. Its scope is local. | 59, 64 |
| logic error | An error in logic that makes the program produce incorrect output. It is up to the programmer to find these types of errors with thorough testing and the use of a robust test plan. | 30 |
| logical operators | The operators are AND, OR, NOT, used in expressions. | 80 |
| lowest value | In an input-loop, programs can find the lowest value entered. | 124 |

| method | Another name for module or function used in object-oriented programming. | 145, 148, 151, 152 |
|---|---|---|
| module | A group of lines of code that are called and executed. | 53, 54, 57 |
| module header | The first line of a group of lines of code that are called and executed. | 54 |
| modulus | A mathematical operator that results in the remainder. Example: 10 MOD 3 = 1   (10/3 = 3 with 1 left over) | 89 |
| naming standards | Variables are named with nouns using the camelCase naming standard. Constants are named with nouns with the uppercase naming standard LIKE_THIS. Modules, functions, and methods are named with a verb using camelCase. | 40-41, 57 |
| nested | Coding structures, such as if-statements and loops, can be nested inside each other. | 79, 105 |
| nested loops | Loops can be nested inside each other. Commonly used with two-dimensional arrays. | 105, 137 |
| no-arg constructor | A constructor with no arguments. An example:  Dog myDog = New Dog () | 147 |
| NOT | A Logical operator used to reverse true or false values. | 80, 81 |
| numeric literal | Values such as:  -3, 0, 42 | 41 |
| object | An object is created from the Class. Contains data and methods. | 145-159 |
| off-by-one error | This occurs when the index accessing an array is outside the bounds of the array. For example: when a program tries to access an array with 5 elements with array[5]. | 136 |
| one-dimensional array | A single list of values stored in an array. | 132-136 |
| one-function input validation routine | The simplest input validation routine. Used when the condition being tested contains no more than 1 Logical operator. | 124-125 |
| OR | A Logical operator used to combine conditions. | 80-81 |
| outOfBoundsError | This occurs when the index accessing an array is outside the bounds of the array. For example: when a program tries to access an array with 5 elements with array[5]. | 134, 136 |
| output | This is what the program creates. Output could be text displayed on the screen, a file the program creates, sound, pictures, or just about anything. | 35, 36, 42 |

| | | |
|---|---|---|
| overloading | Overloading a method enables several methods to have the same name, but with different number or types of parameters. | 152 |
| overriding | Used with a subclass has a method with the same name as the superclass. The subclass's method overrides the superclass's. | 151 |
| parameters | Data passed to a module or function. See Arguments. | 55, 56 |
| pass by reference | This refers to passing a variable to a module or function so the code inside the module or function can update the variable's value. In Java this is only possible for arrays. | 64 |
| pass by value | This refers to passing the value of a variable to a module or function so the variable is local in scope. The code inside the module of function cannot change the original variable in the calling routine. | 64 |
| polymorphism | An object's ability to take on many forms. | 146, 158, 159 |
| patterns | Reusable solutions to commonly occurring problems in software design. | 23 |
| populate | Another word for initialize. Commonly used referring to initializing arrays. | 40 |
| post-test loop | A loop where the code inside the loop is always executed at least once because the test occurs after the code in the loop is excuted. | 99, 100 |
| pre-test loop | A loop where the test occurs before the code to be executed. The code inside the loop may not be executed at all. | 99, 100 |
| priming read | Input done before entering a loop. Commonly used with a sentinel. | 102 |
| private fields | Variables in a class are set to private so other programs can't update them directly | 145, 147 |
| problem-solving techniques | Techniques used to solve problems. Staring at a problem is not effective. Active thinking is required to solve problems. | 29, 49, 116 |
| processing | Part of the Input-Processing-Output program structure. | 45, 47, 66 |
| prompt | Asking or telling the user something before demanding they input a value. | 43 |
| pseudocode | Code that is conceptual and not executable. Used to talk about program structure and programming concepts. | 14, 23, 39 |

| | | |
|---|---|---|
| public methods | Methods that are public so other programs can use public methods to get or set fields in that program | 145, 148 |
| real numbers | Decimal numbers such as: -3.12, -1, 0, 2.22, 17 | 40, 42 |
| real variable type | Used when declaring a real number. Example: Declare Real myRealNumber = 0.0 | 40, 42 |
| return | Used to return from a function to the calling statement. Usually returns a value. | 53, 56, 61 |
| return variable type | The variable type of the variable being returned from a function to the calling statement. | 56, 57 |
| rubber ducky technique | Talking about a problem out loud, even to a yellow rubber duck, gets ideas out of your head and helps produce solutions. | 28-29 |
| total | A total that is accumulated either while the user is entering data, or when looping through an array. | 138 |
| scope | Refers to where a variable or constant can be used. See *global* and *local*. | 54, 59 |
| search | Used to find a value in an array. | 135, 136, 138 |
| Select | A conditional programming structure that uses case-statements to determine which lines of code to execute. | 87 |
| sentinel | An inputted value that tells the program to stop and do something else. | 101. 102, 103, 124, 125, 126 |
| setter | A module. A program calls a setter to set a field to a value | 145, 148 |
| String literals | Examples: "Test" or "What is your name?" | 41 |
| String variable type | A variable that contains a text value such as: "Test" | 42 |
| Strings | Text such as: "Test" | 42, 84, 127 |
| subclass | The specialized class, such as Beagle. Beagle extends Dog. | 146, 149, 150, 151, 155 |
| subscript | Used to access a specific element in an array. For example, to access the first element in an array: myArray[0]. The 0 is the subscript. | 133, 134, 137 |
| superclass | The general class, such as Dog is the superclass of Beagle. | 145, 149, 150, 151, 155 |

| | | |
|---|---|---|
| syntax error | An error caught be the compiler or translator because it does not understand what you wrote. Could be a typo. | 30 |
| test plans | A list of input values with the expected output values. Best created before writing any code. | 34, 128 |
| test values | Values used to test a program. Good programmers are great testers. | 36, 128 |
| testing | During and after coding, programmers test their program to verify it does what they expect it to do. Without testing a programmer cannot know if their program works or not. | 31-36, 128 |
| this | Refers to the object variable or object method to distinguish it from a local variable or method of the same name. | 149 |
| two-dimensional array | Refers to a two-dimensional array. A two-dimensional array can be thought of as containing rows and columns. | 134, 137-140 |
| two-function input validation routine | Used when the condition being tested contains more than 1 Logical operator. It calls a function such as isInvalid(...) that returns a true value when the inputted value is invalid. Returns false when the value is acceptable. | 125-126 |
| UML | Unified Modeling Language. Like IPO Charts and Hierarchy Charts, UML is used to design a program | 145, 153 |
| upperCase | Constants are named using UPPER_CASE in this book. Constants do not change value during program execution. | 40-41, 67 |
| variable | A named location in memory. A variable can change value while the program is executed. | 40-42, 44 |
| wantsToContinue loop | A standard loop that asks the user if they want to continue. Commonly wants a Y or N response. Also called a do-it-again-loop. | 103 |
| while-loop | A pre-test loop. The contents of the loop may not be executed if the condition is initially false. | 99, 100, 102 |
| != | Not Equal to | 78 |
| < | Less than | |
| <= | Less than or Equal to | |
| == | Equal to | |
| > | Greater than | |
| >= | Greater than or Equal to | |

# Appendix B:  Problem-Solving Roadmap

This checklist should be used to analyze a problem and what must be done to write code to solve the problem. This is only a starting point.

_____ Read the problem and imagine or review the sample output in detail.

_____ What input do I need from the user?

_____ What is the output of this program? What does it display to the program's user?

_____ Create a test plan. Refer to the Test Plan Checklist.


_____ Do I need constants? Identify any values that don't change.

_____ Declare constants above main to make them global when appropriate

_____ What kind of constants are they? (Real, Integer, String, Character, Boolean)


_____ Write Display statements asking for the user to enter a value such as a number

_____ Write Input statements, making up appropriate variable names

_____ At the top of the module, declare the variables you just created

_____ What kind of variables are they? (Real, Integer, String, Character, Boolean)


_____ What must happen to the input data to create the output?

_____ Write the formulas that will calculate the values to be displayed as output


_____ Write output Display Statements and make up variable names if necessary

_____ At the top of the module declare the variables from the Display statements you just wrote

_____ What kind of variables are they? (Real, Integer, String, Character, Boolean)


_____ Verify the program statements are in their proper order:  Input / Processing / Output


_____ Use the Program Checklist

# Appendix C:
# Test Plan Checklist

Below is a checklist to use when evaluating a test plan. This is a general checklist—your program may require more specific values to test.

_____ The test plan is formatted appropriately. Your name and the assignment are at the top. Make it look good. Take pride in your work.

_____ All sets of valid and invalid input data for the specific problem are listed as test cases. All types of output conditions are documented.

_____ Each test case tests a different aspect of the input data. In other words, tests do not repeat testing the same type of data. For example, testing input of 4, 5, and 6 as valid months may not be necessary.

_____ Boundary conditions are tested. For example, the test cases for a numeric month should include 0, 1, 12, and 13.

_____ Testing all types of data based on the type of data being input.
For strings, test: null and spaces.
For numbers, test: null, spaces, ABC, 0, -1, 1, 999999, 3.14

_____ Error messages for invalid data are specific and identify the error encountered for the user.

_____ What could go wrong? Test for any other output situations that could occur for this specific problem and verify the program handles them correctly.

_____ Test various combinations of data: bad data and then good data. Bad data twice and then good data. Try to break the code as if you hated the programmer and you want to get them fired for writing crappy code.

# Appendix D:
# Program Checklist

Below is a checklist to use when evaluating a program. This is a general checklist—your program may require more specific items to test. Some items you will not be able to do until we have read the applicable chapter and discussed their usage.

When you turn in a program, you should already know what your grade will be based on the results of the below checklist.

_____  Identifying comments are at the top of the program:
   //  Your name
   //   The assignment

_____  The code is indented consistently in a standard manner.

_____  Blank lines are used in the program to improve readability.

_____  The program is documented with descriptive comments that do not just repeat the code.

_____  When starting, the program explains what the program will do.

_____  The program displays a message indicating it has finished.

_____  The program follows IPO structure.

_____  Variables are declared correctly and named using the camelCase naming standard.

_____  Variables are named appropriately for their purpose using nouns.

_____  Boolean variables are named for the state they represent (isOn, isNotOn, isAlive, isDead, or studentExists, for example).

_____  No unapproved global variables. Global constants are OK.

_____  Constants are declared and named using the UPPER_CASE naming standard.

_____  Constants are named appropriately for their purpose using nound.

_____  ALL numbers in the problem statement are declared as constants.

_____  The program uses all the assignment's required elements such as loops, select statements, compound if statements, arrays, and/or classes and driver programs.

_____  The code is efficient. For example, inefficient code would be a long nested if statement that could have been written in one short line instead.

_____ The program should not crash for any reason. The most common reason programs crash is because they do not handle invalid input data. Test entering non-numeric data for numeric fields!

_____ The program does not use any coding concepts we have not covered yet. If we have not covered these then don't use them: Arraylists, enum, Arrays.sort , Collections.sort.

_____ The program works as required.

_____ Error messages tell the user all the program knows.

_____ There is a minimum amount of code in main. Main should contain code such as variable and constant declaration and initialization statements, function and module calls, a continuation loop, and program control statements such as if or select statements. If related code could be put in a module or function, it should be.

_____ Has too much code been moved from a function? Did moving code leave nothing to do for the calling module?

_____ Modules or functions are used wherever possible and are appropriately named for what they do and they use verbs in their names showing the action they do.

_____ Generalized functions are used whenever possible and appropriate.  Look for duplicate code and generalize it into a function or module.

_____ Program uses the generalized input routines such as getString(..), getInteger(...), and getYesOrNo(...).

_____ The program uses standard One or Two-Function Input Validation routines. The program did not try to 'improve' them by adding more if-statements or while-loops.

_____ Every module and function has comments before it describing the purpose of the module. Parameters are documented.

_____ Functions and modules are called with the correct syntax. Function and module headers are written with the correct syntax.

_____ Returned values from functions are used and not ignored.

_____ Each module or function performs one well-defined task. If the documentation says the function does A and B, then the function should be divided into 2 functions.

_____ Input validation must prevent invalid and nonsensical input.

_____ Input validation routines allow for flexible input such as allowing these values for yes: y, Y, Yes, YES, yes, etc...

# Appendix E:
# Checklist of Coding Concepts

Below is a checklist of basic coding concepts and skills you must master. Once you know these basic building blocks, you will able to create more complicated programs and exhibit the creativity you have inside you. Your ability to write great code advances by extending the number of coding concepts you can use without having to think about how to use them.

_____ 1. Variables are in camelCase and are named appropriately with nouns

_____ 2. Constants are in UPPER_CASE and are named appropriately with nouns

_____ 3. Variables and constants are declared with appropriate variable types

_____ 4. The program's code is properly indented

_____ 5. The program follows IPO structure

_____ 6. Can create a test plan with all appropriate values for valid and invalid data

_____ 7. Can create a Hierarchy Chart

_____ 8. Can create an IPO Chart

_____ 9. Modules and Functions are named appropriated with verbs

_____ 10. Modules and Functions do ONE thing and ONE thing only

_____ 11. Can create a generalized getInteger (...) function

_____ 12. Can create a generalized getString (...) function

_____ 13. Can create a generalized getReal (...) function

_____ 14. Can create a generalized getYesOrNo (...) function

_____ 15. Can write Select-Case statements

_____ 16. Can create a Wants-To-Continue-loop

_____ 17. Can create an Input loop with a Sentinel

_____ 18. Can create an Input loop with unique numbers with a Sentinel

_____ 19. Can create an Input loop with a Sentinel to sum numbers

_____ 20. Can create an Input loop with a Sentinel to average numbers

_____ 21. Can create an Input loop with a Sentinel to count the numbers

_____ 22. Can create an Input loop with a Sentinel to find the lowest number

_____ 23. Can create an Input loop with a Sentinel to find the highest number

_____ 24. Can create an Input loop with a Sentinel to find the number of even numbers

_____ 25. Can create an Input loop with a Sentinel to find the number of odd numbers

_____ 26. Can create Game Loops

_____ 27. Can create a One-Function Input Validation routine

_____ 28. Can create a Two-Function Input Validation routine

_____ 29. Can create and use parallel arrays

Can do the following for a One-Dimensional Array:

    _____ 30. Initialize a one-dimensional array with unique entered numbers

    _____ 31. Initialize a one-dimensional array with unique random numbers

    _____ 32. Print a one-dimensional array horizontally with a separator such as a comma

    _____ 33. Print a one-dimensional array vertically

    _____ 34. Search a one-dimensional array

Can do the following for a Two-Dimensional Array:

    _____ 35. Initialize a two-dimensional array with unique entered numbers

    _____ 36. Initialize a two-dimensional array with unique random numbers

    _____ 37. Print a two-dimensional array

    _____ 38. Search a two-dimensional array

OOP concepts:

    _____ 39. Can write UML to define a class

    _____ 40. Can create OOP super-class: Animal

    _____ 41. Can create OOP sub-classes Dog and Cat that extends Animal

    _____ 42. Can create OOP sub-class Beagle to extend Dog

    _____ 43. Can create an OOP driver program to create Animal, Dog, Cat, Beagle objects

    _____ 44. Can create a method in the OOP driver program to demonstrate polymorphism

Check off each concept as you master each of them. If you can code all the above, you are ready for anything your next computer science class has to throw at you.

Congratulations on your expertise!

# Appendix F:
# Using Computer Science Tutors

Tutors are valuable additions to the classroom. They can help you bridge gaps in your knowledge and help you get back up to speed when you miss a class. You are encouraged to meet with a tutor whenever you are stuck or need a little more explanation of a problem-solving or coding concept.

General guidelines:

- Students who use tutors should NOT ask a tutor to "help with my homework." That is too general a request.
- Students who use tutors should NOT see a tutor when they have not even read the assigned chapter.
- Students who use tutors should NOT expect a tutor to write ANY code for them.
- Students should use tutors to learn more about the subject matter discussed in the class and in textbooks.
- Students should use tutors to help them understand a problem-solving or coding technique.
- Students should use tutors to help them understand the concepts, after which you will find the homework easy to complete.

**Grading Philosophy:** If a homework assignment requires a For-loop, for example, and you have not done the reading and has not studied For loops, you ***will not be able*** to do the homework. You ***SHOULD*** receive a failing grade for that assignment. Don't expect a tutor to bail you out from not knowing the material.

Expectations of Students meeting with tutors:

- When you are doing a homework assignment, you should have created a test plan to test your program before writing any code. Your test plan should be extremely clear—it should be easy enough for your grandmother to enter in the required input with prompts from the program and then to examine the expected and actual output and tell you if the program worked or not. The test plan should tell your grandmother the exact values to enter.

- If you cannot write pseudocode demonstrating how a concept is used, you don't understand the concept. Too many students use the compiler to work out errors in their thinking via a trial-and-error process instead of learning the concepts to begin with. This wastes their time and the tutor's time.

- You must not use coding concepts we have not covered in class yet, such as arrays, lists, slices, arraylists, enums, or try-catch blocks. When this happens, it's clear the student received code from other people and did not write the code themselves. That's cheating.

If you want help understanding a coding concept:
- Before meeting with a tutor, be sure to read the applicable section of the textbook.
- Be prepared to show the tutor the section of the textbook that is confusing you.
- Be prepared to describe in English what you are trying to do.

# Appendix G:
# Tutoring Computer Science Students

Tutors are valuable additions to the classroom. They can help students bridge gaps in their knowledge and help students get back up to speed when they miss a class. Students are encouraged to meet with a tutor whenever they are stuck or need a little more explanation of a problem-solving or coding concept.

Unfortunately, too many students have admitted they could not write any code in class because they relied on tutors too much to help them get through the assignments. Those student's tutors did a real disservice to those students who are now going to have a very tough time in their future coding classes.

If students cannot do the assignments, they should fail the class. It is not the tutor's job to bail out students from their lack of participation in their own education.

Tutors should not prevent students from failing by writing a For-loop for the student's assignment when the student cannot write one on their own. Students must take responsibility for their own education and do the required reading and learn the required concepts *before* starting their assignments.

Tutors should…

- Encourage students to start their assignments at least a week before the assignment is due.
- Encourage students to follow the process of analysis, design, and then coding and testing.
- Discourage students from thinking this class as a class in coding—it's a class in solving problems.
- Not write even one line of code for the student. Don't point at the code on their screen and tell them what to type. Instead, point at the examples in the textbook and let the student apply what they learn to their assignment. Yes, the student will take longer to finish an assignment. But, learning *takes* time.
- If the student asks, "Is this right?", don't answer. Encourage the student to determine if the code is correct or not by letting them test it—either by desk-checking the code or by running the program. Let the student have their 'ah-ha' moment when their code works, or it doesn't.

- If a student wants help on an assignment:
  - Help the student walk through the process of analysis and design before starting any coding. If they come for help, they should have a completed test plan, a Hierarchy chart or a detailed IPO chart. If they say they don't have time for that, then they don't have time to meet the assignment's deadline. Encourage the student to start the next assignment sooner. Let that be a lesson for them.

  - If the student wants help in writing some code, ask to see the student's test plan. If they don't have one, or the test plan they have is inadequate to test their program, work with the student to create the test plan and a Hierarchy chart or a detailed IPO chart before writing any code. Don't let the student code without thinking about the problem in detail.

- Once the test plan is adequate and they have designed the program with a Hierarchy chart or a detailed IPO chart, the student can start to write their program.

- If the student makes syntax errors, have the student look up the syntax themselves. Having the student look up information in the textbook enables the student to be more comfortable with the textbook and its contents.

- Once the pseudocode is desk-checked, the student can then convert it to a programming language such as Java or Python and begin the cycle of coding, compiling, testing, and fixing bugs.

- You can help the student use the coding evaluation checklist to review their code and pointing out what does not meet the basic requirements.


- If a student wants help understanding a concept:
    - Ask the student to show you in the textbook which section is confusing them. Expect the student to have studied the appropriate textbook section before coming to you.

    - If they have not read the textbook yet, ask them to return after they have read the required text.

    - If the student has done the reading but is still not getting it, give them examples and whatever help you can—just don't use the homework assignment in your examples.


And a big thank you to all the tutors who help students learn and grow in their abilities and understanding!

# Appendix H:
# Pseudocode to Java Examples

| Pseudocode Examples | Java Examples |
|---|---|
| Declare String name<br>Declare Integer price<br>Declare Boolean overtime<br>Declare Real cost<br>Declare Real cost | String name;<br>int price;<br>boolean overtime;<br>float cost;<br>double cost; |
| Constant Integer SIZE = 5 | final int SIZE = 5; |
| Set name = "Bob"<br>Set price = 20;<br>Set overtime = true<br>Set cost = price + tax<br><br>*(note: "set" is optional)* | *(assuming the variables have already been declared)*<br>name = "Bob";<br>price = 20;<br>overtime = true;<br>cost = price + tax;<br>----- *or declare the variables when first used* -----<br>String name = "Bob"<br>int price = 20;<br>boolean overtime = true;<br>float cost = price + tax; |
| Display "My name is ", name<br>Display "Error" | System.out.println("My name is " + name);<br>System.err.println("Error");  //prints in red |
| Input name | Scanner keyboard = New Scanner(System.in);<br>answer = keyboard.nextLine();<br>---------------------------- *or* -----<br>InputStreamReader input = new<br>                    InputStreamReader(System.in);<br>BufferedReader reader = New BufferedReader(input);<br><br>try {<br>   name = reader.readLine();<br>}<br>catch (Exception e) {<br>   System.err.println("Error reading input.");<br>   System.exit(-1);<br>} |
| Call displayReport("Hi") | displayReport("Hi"); |
| Module displayReport<br>          (String message)<br>   // code goes here<br>End Module | private static void displayReport (String message) {<br>   // code goes here<br>} |
| Declare String myString<br>myString = getString(msg) | String myString = getString(msg); |

| | |
|---|---|
| `Function String getString`<br>`            (String message)`<br>`    //code goes here`<br>`    Return name`<br>`End Function` | `private static String getString (String message) {`<br>`    //code goes here`<br>`    return name;`<br>`}` |
| `If x == 4` | `if (x == 4) {` |
| `If myString == "test"` | `if (myString.equals("test")) {` |
| `If a > 0 AND a < 100` | `if (a > 0 && a < 100) {` |
| `If a < 0 OR a > 100` | `if (a < 0 || a > 100) {` |
| `For x = 1 to 100 Step 1` | `for (int x = 1; x <= 100; x++) {` |
| `Declare Integer months[12]`<br>`Declare String names[20]` | `int [ ] months = New int[12];`<br>`String [ ] names = New String [20];` |

Some Java and coding concepts to remember:

- Lines of code end in a semi-colon like this: `int x = y + z;`

- Java requires *brackets* around coding blocks: { //code goes here  }
  A good method to keep brackets straight is to always type the starting and ending brackets at the same time and then go back and fill in the code between them.

- When the Java compiler shows you an error message with a line number, sometimes the actual line with the error is the line above that line number.

- The variable type int is not the same as Integer. Use int unless you have a reason not to.

- The variable type boolean is not the same as Boolean. Use boolean.

- When writing and reading code, make the font size the biggest you can and still see a significant number of lines. There is a reason why software developers use BIG screens. When you are looking for ";" instead of "," a big font size will help you find the error.

- Before writing a program, you must know what you are trying write! Sitting in front of your computer is not a good time to design your program.

- Just because the program compiles does not mean it is correct.

- Just because the program ran without crashing does not mean it does what it is supposed to do. Look at your program output with fresh eyes to see the errors.

# Appendix I:
# Pseudocode to Python Examples

| Pseudocode Examples | Python Examples |
|---|---|
| Declare String name<br>Declare Integer price<br>Declare Boolean overtime<br>Declare Real cost<br>Declare Real cost | *Declaring a variable type is not necessary in Python* |
| Constant Integer SIZE = 5 | SIZE = 5 |
| Set name = "Bob"<br>Set price = 20;<br>Set overtime = true<br>Set cost = price + tax<br><br>*(note: "set" is optional)* | name = 'Bob'<br>price = 20<br>overtime = true<br>cost = price + tax |
| Display "My name is ", name<br>Display "Error" | print ('My name is ', name)<br>print ('Error')<br>print                    //goes to a new line |
| Input name | name = raw_input() |
| Call displayReport("Hi") | displayReport('Hi') |
| Module displayReport<br>          (String message)<br>    // code goes here<br>End Module | def displayReport (message)<br>    // code goes here<br>// The next un-indented line ends the module |
| Declare String myString<br>myString = getString(msg) | //Python does not need to declare variable types<br>myString = getString(msg) |
| Function String getString<br>          (String message)<br>    Return name<br>End Function | def getString (message)<br>    // code goes here<br>    return name<br>// The next un-indented line ends the module |
| If x == 4 | if x == 4 |
| If myString == "test" | if myString == 'test' |
| If a > 0 AND a < 100 | if a > 0 and a < 100 |
| If a < 0 OR a > 100 | if a < 0 or a > 100 |
| For x = 1 to 100 Step 1 | for x in myString |
| Declare Integer months[12]<br>Declare String names[20] | *Declaring variable types is not necessary in Python* |

Some Python and coding concepts to remember:

- Python requires indentions to be correct.

- Python uses lists and slices instead of arrays. They are very similar to arrays.

- When writing and reading code, make the font size the biggest you can and still see a significant number of lines. There is a reason why software developers use BIG screens. When you are looking for ";" instead of "," a big font size will help you find the error.

- Before writing a program, you must know what you are trying write! Sitting in front of your computer is not a good time to design your program.

- Just because the program compiles does not mean it is correct.

- Just because the program ran without crashing does not mean it does what it is supposed to do. Look at your program output with fresh eyes to see the errors.

**----- Quote References -----**

"Nathaniel Borenstein." AZQuotes.com. Wind and Fly LTD, 2019. 08 July 2019.
https://www.azquotes.com/quote/611649"

"Mark Van Doren." AZQuotes.com. Wind and Fly LTD, 2019. 08 July 2019.
https://www.azquotes.com/quote/539640

"Thomas A. Edison." AZQuotes.com. Wind and Fly LTD, 2019. 08 July 2019.
https://www.azquotes.com/quote/86497

"Albert Einstein." AZQuotes.com. Wind and Fly LTD, 2019. 08 July 2019. https://www.azquotes.com/quote/373439

"Martin Fowler." AZQuotes.com. Wind and Fly LTD, 2019. 08 July 2019. https://www.azquotes.com/quote/580953

"R. Buckminster Fuller." AZQuotes.com. Wind and Fly LTD, 2019. 08 July 2019.
https://www.azquotes.com/quote/104087

"Martin Golding." softwarequotes.com. 2019. 08 July 2019.
https://www.softwarequotes.com/showquotes.aspx?id=617

"Will Rogers." AZQuotes.com. Wind and Fly LTD, 2019. 08 July 2019. https://www.azquotes.com/quote/349455

"Henry David Thoreau." AZQuotes.com. Wind and Fly LTD, 2019. 08 July 2019.
https://www.azquotes.com/quote/294073

----- **Notes** -----

----- **Notes** -----

----- **Notes** -----

 **David A. Freitag** worked in computer software development for more than twenty-five years. He started as a programmer and moved up to programmer/analyst, team leader, programming supervisor, product manager, project manager, and eventually became a Director in a large software company in San Francisco, California during the dot-com era.

He has written and published games for both Android phones and Windows desktops.

He now teaches programming courses to the next generation of software developers in the Computer Science department at Pima Community College in Tucson, Arizona.

Visit the author's website at: www.dafreitag.com

Contact the author at: dafreitag@pima.edu or freitag2us@comcast.net


Android Games:

*Gemini Falcon: Asteroid Miner*

*Gemini Falcon: All Boxed In*

*RPSLS: Rock, Paper, Scissors, Lizard, Spook*

*Ay Caramba!*

*The Oracle*


Other books by David A. Freitag:

*Too Shy to Speak*

*The Choate Family: 1900-1999*

*Create. Share. Repeat.*

*The Sword in the Machine: A Tom Turing Mystery*

Made in the USA
Columbia, SC
31 December 2019